KEEP
CALM
AND
BAKE
CUPCAKES

KEEP CALM

AND

BAKE CUPCAKES

THUNDER BAY
P·R·E·S·S

Thunder Bay Press
An imprint of the Baker & Taylor Publishing Group
10350 Barnes Canyon Road, San Diego, CA 92121
www.thunderbaybooks.com

ISBN-13: 978-1-60710-925-9
ISBN-10: 1-60710-925-5

Library of Congress Cataloging-in-Publication Data

Dixon, Barbara (Barbara Elizabeth)
  Keep calm and bake cupcakes / Barbara Dixon.
    pages cm
  ISBN 978-1-60710-925-9 -- ISBN 1-60710-925-5
  1. Cupcakes. I. Title.
  TX771.D48 2013
  641.86'5--dc23

                    2013024469

Printed in China

2 3 4 5 17 16 15 14

Cover illustration by Emma Kelly

Photographers: Steve Baxter (pages 96 and 185); Nicki Dowey (pages 11, 29, 149, 151, 155, 157, 160, 203, 209, 211, 214, 215, 219, 221, 223, and 225); William Lingwood (pages 24, 39, 61, 80, 88, 101, 105, 107, 110, 112, 117, 152, 163, 168, 173, 189, 190, 193, 135, 136, 201, 207, and 233); Myles New (pages 159 and 227); Craig Robertson (pages 126, 208, and 218); Sam Stowell (page 226); Lucinda Symons (pages 9, 10, 15, 18, 21, 26, 30, 31, 32, 35, 51, 52, 63, 64, 65, 66, 69, 70, 71, 72, 95, 115, 127, 141, 148, 158, 161, 165, 169, 170, 177, 178, 180, 181, 189, 202, 213, and 222); Philip Webb (page 217); Kate Whitaker (page 175); Rachel Whiting (pages 13, 16, 23, 37, 41, 42, 45, 47, 54, 57, 58, 75, 76, 79, 85, 87, 91, 93, 99, 103, 109, 119, 121, 123, 129, 131, 132, 135, 137, 139, 143, 145, 146, 186, 199, 229, 230, 235, and 236)

Home Economists: Joanna Farrow, Emma Jane Frost, Teresa Goldfinch, Alice Hart, Lucy McKelvie, Kim Morphew, Bridget Sargeson, and Mari Mererid Williams

Stylists: Tamzin Ferdinando, Lizzie Harris, Wei Tang, Helen Trent, and Fanny Ward

Notes
All spoon measures are level.
1 teaspoon = 5ml spoon; 1 tablespoon = 15ml spoon.
Ovens and broilers must be preheated to the specified temperature.
Large eggs should be used except where otherwise specified.

Dietary Guidelines
Note that certain recipes contain raw or lightly cooked eggs. The young, elderly, pregnant women, and anyone with immune-deficiency disease should avoid these because of the slight risk of salmonella.
Note that some recipes contain alcohol. Check the ingredients list before serving to children.

Contents

CUPCAKES WITH A TWIST

Breakfast Cupcakes

Preparation Time 30 minutes • Cooking Time 20 minutes, plus cooling and setting • Makes 12 •
Per Cupcake 327 calories, 14g fat (8g saturated), 48g carbohydrates, 300mg sodium • Easy

¾ cup (1½ sticks) unsalted butter,
  softened
½ cup superfine sugar
3 large eggs
¼ cup plus 2 teaspoons apricot
  preserves
1⅛ cups plus 4 teaspoons all-
  purpose flour, sifted
¾ cup oat bran
1½ teaspoons baking powder

FOR THE TOPPING
2 cups confectioners' sugar
1–2 tablespoons orange juice
¾ cup mixed berry granola

1. Preheat the oven to 375°F. Line a 12-cup muffin pan with paper muffin liners.

2. Using a hand mixer, beat the butter and superfine sugar in a bowl, or beat with a wooden spoon, until pale and creamy. Gradually beat in the eggs until just combined. Using a metal spoon, fold in the apricot preserves, flour, oat bran, and baking powder until combined. Divide the batter equally between the paper liners.

3. Bake for 20 minutes or until golden and risen. Leave to cool in the pan for 5 minutes, and then transfer to a wire rack to cool completely.

4. For the topping, sift the confectioners' sugar into a bowl, and then add enough orange juice to achieve a smooth, thick icing. Spoon a little on top of each cake, and then sprinkle with the granola. Stand the cupcakes upright on the wire rack and leave for about 1 hour to set.

TO STORE
Store in an airtight container. They will keep for 3–5 days.

FREEZING TIP
__To freeze__ Complete the recipe to the end of step 3. Open-freeze, and then wrap and freeze.
__To use__ Thaw for about 1 hour, and then complete the recipe.

Toast and Marmalade Cupcakes

Preparation Time 30 minutes • Cooking Time 20–25 minutes, plus cooling and setting • Makes 12 •
Per Cupcake 336 calories, 10g fat (2g saturated), 57g carbohydrates, 1,500mg sodium • Easy

⅔ cup low-fat olive oil spread
1½ cups plus 2 tablespoons
   all-purpose whole-wheat flour,
   sifted
1¼ teaspoons baking powder
¾ cup packed light brown sugar
⅛ cup plus 2 teaspoons
   marmalade
⅓ cup plus 1 tablespoon milk
zest of 1 unwaxed orange (see
   Cook's Tip on page 162)
1 cup fresh whole-wheat bread
   crumbs

FOR THE TOPPING
⅓ cup marmalade
2⅔ cups confectioners' sugar,
   sifted

1. Preheat the oven to 350°F. Line a 12-cup muffin pan with paper muffin liners.

2. Put the low-fat spread, flour, baking powder, brown sugar, eggs, marmalade, milk, orange zest, and bread crumbs into a large bowl. Using a hand mixer, beat together until pale and creamy. Divide the batter equally between the paper liners.

3. Bake for 20–25 minutes until golden and risen. Leave to cool in the pan for 5 minutes, and then transfer to a wire rack to cool completely.

4. For the topping, pass the marmalade through a strainer into a bowl to remove the rind. Reserve the rind. Mix the confectioners' sugar with the strained marmalade in a bowl until it forms a smooth icing. Spoon a little icing onto each cake to flood the top, and then sprinkle with the reserved rind. Stand the cakes upright on the wire rack and leave for about 1 hour to set.

TO STORE
Store in an airtight container. They will keep for 3–5 days.

FREEZING TIP
To freeze *Complete the recipe to the end of step 3. Open-freeze, and then wrap and freeze.*
To use *Thaw for about 1 hour, and then complete the recipe.*

Vanilla and White Chocolate Cupcakes

Preparation Time 25 minutes • Cooking Time 15–20 minutes, plus cooling and setting • Makes 12 •
Per Cupcake 270 calories, 15g fat (9g saturated), 32g carbohydrates, 200mg sodium • Easy

½ cup (1 stick) unsalted butter, at
   room temperature
½ cup plus 2 tablespoons superfine
   sugar
1 vanilla bean
2 large eggs
1 cup all-purpose flour, sifted
1 teaspoon baking powder
1 teaspoon vanilla extract

FOR THE TOPPING

7 ounces white chocolate, broken
   into pieces
12 crystallized violets or frosted
   flowers (see Cook's Tip)

1. Preheat the oven to 375°F.
Line a 12-cup muffin pan with paper
muffin liners.

2. Put the butter and sugar into
a bowl. Split the vanilla bean
lengthwise, scrape out the seeds,
and add to the bowl. Add the eggs,
flour, baking powder, and vanilla
extract and then, using a hand
mixer, mix thoroughly until smooth
and creamy. Spoon the batter into
the paper liners.

3. Bake for 15–20 minutes until
pale golden, risen, and springy
to the touch. Leave in the pan for
2–3 minutes. Then transfer to a
wire rack to cool completely.

4. For the topping, melt the
chocolate in a heatproof bowl set
over a pan of gently simmering
water, making sure the bottom of
the bowl doesn't touch the water.
Stir until smooth and leave to cool
slightly. Spoon the chocolate onto
the cakes and top with a frosted
flower. Stand the cakes upright
on the wire rack and leave for
about 1 hour to set.

TO STORE
*Store in an airtight container. They
will keep for 3–5 days.*

FREEZING TIP
To freeze *Complete the recipe
to the end of step 3. Open-freeze,
and then wrap and freeze.*
To use *Thaw for about 1 hour,
and then complete the recipe.*

COOK'S TIP
*To make the frosted flowers, whisk
1 large egg white in a clean bowl
for 30 seconds or until frothy. Brush
it over 12 violet petals and put on
a wire rack. Lightly dust with
superfine sugar and leave to dry.*

Pomegranate Cupcakes

Preparation Time 30 minutes • Cooking Time 15–20 minutes, plus cooling • Makes 12 •
Per Cupcake 561 calories, 20g fat (12g saturated), 82g carbohydrates, 400mg sodium • Easy

¾ cup (1½ sticks) unsalted butter,
   at room temperature
¾ cup plus 2 tablespoons superfine
   sugar
3 large eggs
1⅓ cups plus 1 tablespoon all-
   purpose flour, sifted
1¼ teaspoons baking powder
1 tablespoon unsweetened cocoa
   powder, sifted
juice and seeds of 1 pomegranate

FOR THE TOPPING
⅔ cup cream cheese
5¼ cups confectioners' sugar,
   sifted
juice and seeds of 1 pomegranate

1. Preheat the oven to 350°F. Line a 12-cup muffin pan with paper muffin liners.

2. Using a hand mixer, beat the butter and superfine sugar in a bowl, or beat with a wooden spoon, until pale and creamy. Gradually beat in the eggs until just combined.

3. Fold in the flour, baking powder, cocoa powder, and pomegranate juice and stir well to combine. Fold in the pomegranate seeds. Divide the batter evenly among the paper liners and bake for 15–20 minutes until risen and springy to the touch. Transfer to a wire rack to cool completely.

4. For the topping, place the cream cheese in a medium bowl and stir with a fork to soften. Gradually add the sifted confectioners' sugar, stirring well until incorporated. Add the pomegranate juice and beat until well combined. Transfer to a pastry bag fitted with a large star tip.

5. Pipe a swirl of pomegranate cream onto the top of each cake. Sprinkle the pomegranate seeds over each cake to decorate.

Mini Green Tea Cupcakes

Preparation Time 40 minutes • Cooking Time 25 minutes, plus cooling and infusing • Makes 12 minis •
Per Cupcake 282 calories, 13g fat (8g saturated), 41g carbohydrates, 300mg sodium • Easy

⅓ cup plus 1 tablespoon milk

2 teaspoons loose green tea leaves

7 tablespoons unsalted butter,
    softened

½ cup plus 2 tablespoons
    superfine sugar

2 large eggs

1⅛ cups plus 4 teaspoons all-
    purpose flour, sifted

1¼ teaspoons baking powder

FOR THE TOPPING

3 teaspoons loose green tea leaves

about ⅓ cup boiling water

6 tablespoons unsalted butter,
    softened

2¼ cups confectioners' sugar,
    sifted

store-bought sugar flowers

1. Preheat the oven to 375°F. Line a
12-cup mini muffin pan with paper
liners.

2. Put the milk into a small saucepan
and bring to a boil. Add the green
tea leaves and leave to steep for
30 minutes.

3. Using a hand mixer, beat the
butter and superfine sugar in a
bowl, or beat with a wooden spoon,
until pale and creamy. Gradually
beat in the eggs until just combined.
Pass the green tea milk through a
strainer into the bowl. Discard the
tea leaves. Using a metal spoon,
fold in the flour and baking powder
until combined. Divide the batter
equally between the paper liners.

4. Bake for 18–20 minutes until
golden and risen. Leave to cool
in the pan for 5 minutes, and then
transfer to a wire rack to cool
completely.

5. For the topping, put the green
tea leaves into a bowl, add the
boiling water, and leave to steep
for 5 minutes. Put the butter into a
bowl and beat until fluffy. Gradually
add the confectioners' sugar and
beat until combined. Pass the green
tea through a strainer into the bowl.
Discard the tea leaves. Continue to
beat until light and fluffy.

6. Insert a star tip into a pastry bag,
fill the bag with the buttercream,
and pipe a swirl onto the top of
each cake. Decorate each with
a sugar flower.

TO STORE

*Store in an airtight container. They
will keep for 3–5 days.*

FREEZING TIP

*To freeze Complete the recipe to
the end of step 4. Open-freeze,
then wrap and freeze.*

*To use Thaw for about 1 hour, and
then complete the recipe.*

Red Velvet Cupcakes

Preparation Time 35 minutes • Cooking Time 15–20 minutes, plus cooling • Makes 12 •
Per Cupcake 424 calories, 24g fat (15g saturated), 51g carbohydrates, 300mg sodium • Easy

¾ cup (1½ sticks) unsalted butter,
  at room temperature
¾ cup plus 2 tablespoons superfine
  sugar
3 large eggs
1⅓ cups plus 1 tablespoon all-
  purpose flour, sifted
1¼ teaspoons baking powder
2 tablespoons unsweetened cocoa
  powder
2–4 teaspoons red gel food coloring

FOR THE TOPPING
½ cup (1 stick) unsalted butter,
  at room temperature
2–3 tablespoons warm water
2½ cups confectioners' sugar,
  sifted
red edible glitter
mixed mini sugar hearts

1. Preheat the oven to 350°F. Line a 12-cup muffin pan with paper muffin liners. Using a hand mixer, beat the butter and superfine sugar in a bowl, or beat with a wooden spoon, until pale and creamy. Gradually beat in the eggs until just combined.

2. Fold in the flour, baking powder, and cocoa powder and stir well to combine. Add a couple teaspoons of the gel coloring and stir into the batter. Add more coloring, if necessary, until the batter is a dark red color. Divide the batter evenly among the paper liners and bake for 15–20 minutes until risen and springy to the touch. Transfer to a wire rack to cool completely.

3. For the topping, place the butter in a bowl and cream until soft. Gradually beat the confectioners' sugar plus the warm water into the butter until smooth. Transfer the frosting to a pastry bag fitted with a large star tip and pipe a swirl of frosting onto each cake. Sprinkle the edible glitter all over the cakes and add a sprinkling of edible mixed mini sugar hearts onto the frosting.

Lavender and Honey Cupcakes

Preparation Time 35 minutes • Cooking Time 15–20 minutes, plus cooling and setting • Makes 9 •
Per Cupcake 316 calories, 13g fat (8g saturated), 50g carbohydrates, 300mg sodium • Easy

½ cup (1 stick) unsalted butter, softened
⅓ cup plus 2 teaspoons honey
2 large eggs
1 cup all-purpose flour, sifted
2 teaspoons baking powder

FOR THE TOPPING
3 honey and lavender tea bags
¼ cup water
2 teaspoons unsalted butter
2¼ cups confectioners' sugar, sifted
red and blue food coloring
purple sugar stars
edible silver dust (optional)

1. Preheat the oven to 375°F. Line a 12-cup muffin pan with 9 paper muffin liners.

2. Using a hand mixer, beat the butter and honey in a bowl, or beat with a wooden spoon, until combined. Gradually mix in the eggs until just combined. Using a metal spoon, fold in the flour and baking powder until combined. Divide the batter equally between the paper liners.

3. Bake for 15–20 minutes until golden and risen. Leave to cool in the pan for 5 minutes, and then transfer to a wire rack to cool completely.

4. For the icing, steep the tea bags in the boiling water in a small bowl for 5 minutes. Remove the tea bags and squeeze out the excess water into the bowl. Stir in the butter until melted. Put the confectioners' sugar into a large bowl, add the tea mixture, and stir to make a smooth icing. Add a few drops of blue and red food coloring until it is lilac in color.

5. Spoon a little icing on top of each cake, to flood the tops. Then sprinkle with stars. Stand the cakes upright on the wire rack and leave for about 1 hour to set. Dust with edible dust, if desired, when set.

TO STORE
Store in an airtight container. They will keep for 3–5 days.

FREEZING TIP
To freeze Complete the recipe to the end of step 3. Open-freeze, and then wrap and freeze.
To use Thaw for about 1 hour, and then complete the recipe.

Pistachio and Cornmeal Cupcakes

Preparation Time 35 minutes • Cooking Time 25 minutes, plus cooling • Makes 12 • Per Cupcake 542 calories, 33g fat (13g saturated), 56g carbohydrates, 600mg sodium • Gluten Free • Easy

1 cup shelled pistachio nuts

¾ cup (1½ sticks) unsalted butter, softened

¾ cup plus 2 tablespoons superfine sugar

3 large eggs

1¼ cups finely-ground cornmeal

½ teaspoon baking powder

1⅔ cups ground almonds (almond meal)

zest of 2 unwaxed lemons (see Cook's Tip on page 162)

2 tablespoons milk

FOR THE TOPPING

7 tablespoons unsalted butter, softened

2⅔ cups confectioners' sugar, sifted

juice of 2 lemons

1. Preheat the oven to 350°F. Line a 12-cup muffin pan with paper muffin liners.

2. Whiz the pistachios in a food processor until finely chopped.

3. Using a hand mixer, beat the butter and superfine sugar in a bowl, or beat with a wooden spoon, until pale and creamy. Gradually beat in the eggs until just combined. Using a metal spoon, fold in the cornmeal, baking powder, ground almonds, lemon zest, milk, and ⅔ cup ground pistachios until combined. Divide the batter equally between the paper liners.

4. Bake for 25 minutes or until golden and risen. Leave to cool in the pan for 5 minutes, and then transfer to a wire rack to cool completely.

5. For the topping, put the butter into a bowl and beat until fluffy. Gradually beat in half the confectioners' sugar. Then add the lemon juice and the remaining confectioners' sugar, mixing until light and fluffy. Using a small spatula, spread a little of the buttercream over the top of each cake, and sprinkle with a little of the remaining chopped pistachios.

TO STORE
Store in an airtight container. They will keep for 3–5 days.

FREEZING TIP
To freeze Complete the recipe to the end of step 4. Open-freeze, and then wrap and freeze.
To use Thaw for about 1 hour, and then complete the recipe.

Black Forest Cupcakes

Preparation Time 30 minutes • Cooking Time 15–20 minutes, plus cooling • Makes 12 •
Per Cupcake 389 calories, 28g fat (17g saturated), 32g carbohydrates, 400mg sodium • Easy

1 (16-ounce) can dark pitted
  cherries
¾ cup (1½ sticks) unsalted butter,
  at room temperature
¾ cup plus 2 tablespoons superfine
  sugar
3 large eggs
1⅓ cups plus 1 tablespoon all-
  purpose flour, sifted
1¼ teaspoons baking powder
2 tablespoons unsweetened cocoa
  powder

FOR THE TOPPING

1¼ cups heavy cream
1 tablespoon cherry liqueur or
  Kirsch*
3 tablespoons finely grated
  semisweet chocolate (at least
  70% cocoa solids)

1. Preheat the oven to 350°F. Line a 12-cup muffin pan with paper muffin liners. Drain the cherries and reserve the syrup. Set aside 12 cherries and finely chop the remainder.

2. Using a hand mixer, beat the butter and superfine sugar in a bowl, or beat with a wooden spoon, until pale and creamy. Gradually beat in the eggs until just combined.

3. Fold in the flour, baking powder, cocoa powder, and chopped cherries and stir well to combine. Divide the batter evenly among the paper liners and bake for 15–20 minutes until risen and springy to the touch. Transfer to a wire rack to cool completely.

4. For the topping, whip the cream until soft peaks just form. Add the cherry liqueur or Kirsch to the reserved syrup and stir well. Stir 2 tablespoons of the syrup mixture into the whipped cream. Using a toothpick, make several small holes in the top of each cold cake and drip over a few drops of the reserved syrup.

5. Transfer the cream to a pastry bag fitted with a large star tip and pipe a swirl of cream on each cake. Sprinkle grated chocolate over and top each cake with the remaining reserved cherries.

* This recipe is not suitable for children because it contains alcohol.

Crème de Menthe Cupcakes

Preparation Time 30 minutes • Cooking Time 15–20 minutes, plus cooling • Makes 12 •
Per Cupcake 618 calories, 34g fat (21g saturated), 77g carbohydrates, 400mg sodium • A Little Effort

¾ cup (1½ sticks) unsalted butter,
   at room temperature
¾ cup plus 2 tablespoons superfine
   sugar
3 large eggs
1⅓ cups plus 1 tablespoon all-
   purpose flour, sifted
1¼ teaspoons baking powder
2 tablespoons crème de menthe*
4 ounces semisweet, milk, or white
   mint chocolate, broken into
   pieces
¼–½ teaspoon green gel
   food coloring

FOR THE TOPPING

1 cup (2 sticks) unsalted butter,
   at room temperature
4 cups confectioners' sugar, sifted
4 tablespoons crème de menthe
¼–½ teaspoon green gel food
   coloring
3 ounces semisweet, milk, or white
   mint chocolate, broken into
   pieces
12 leaves of fresh mint (optional)

1. Preheat the oven to 350°F. Line a 12-cup muffin pan with paper muffin liners. Using a hand mixer, beat the butter and superfine sugar in a bowl, or beat with a wooden spoon, until pale and creamy. Gradually beat in the eggs until just combined.

2. Fold in the flour, baking powder, crème de menthe, white chocolate pieces, and green food coloring and stir well to combine. Divide the batter evenly among the paper liners. Bake for 15–20 minutes until golden and risen. Leave to cool in the pan for 5 minutes, and then transfer to a wire rack to cool completely.

3. For the topping, put the butter into a bowl and beat until fluffy. Gradually add the confectioners' sugar, the crème de menthe, and green food coloring and beat until light and fluffy.

4. Transfer the frosting to a pastry bag fitted with a large plain tip and pipe a large swirl on top of each cake. Decorate with a few pieces of the chocolate mint chunks and top with a fresh mint leaf, if using.

This recipe is not suitable for children because it contains alcohol.

Nutty Cupcakes

Preparation Time 40 minutes • Cooking Time 25 minutes, plus cooling and setting • Makes 12 •
Per Cupcake 338 calories, 23g fat (10g saturated), 31g carbohydrates, 400mg sodium • Easy

**10 tablespoons unsalted butter,
softened**
**1⅓ cups plus 1 tablespoon all-
purpose flour, sifted**
¼ cup superfine sugar
**⅓ cup plus 1 tablespoon light corn
syrup**
3 large eggs
2¼ teaspoons baking powder
1 teaspoon apple pie spice
⅓ cup mixed chopped nuts

FOR THE TOPPING
3 tablespoons heavy cream
1 tablespoon milk
**2 ounces milk chocolate, finely
chopped**
**1 ounce semisweet chocolate,
finely chopped**
½ cup roasted chopped hazelnuts

1. Preheat the oven to 375°F. Line a 12-cup muffin pan with paper muffin liners.

2. Put the butter, flour, sugar, syrup, eggs, baking powder, apple pie spice, and nuts into a large bowl. Using a hand mixer, beat together until pale and creamy. Divide the batter equally between the paper liners.

3. Bake for 20 minutes or until golden and risen. Leave to cool in the pan for 5 minutes, and then transfer to a wire rack to cool completely.

4. For the topping, heat the cream and milk in a small saucepan until nearly boiling. Put both chocolates into a bowl and pour the hot cream over them. Leave to stand for 5 minutes, and then gently stir until smooth.

5. Put the hazelnuts into a shallow bowl. Dip the top of each cake into the chocolate cream, allow the excess to drip off, and then dip into the hazelnuts until coated all over. Stand the cakes upright on a wire rack and leave for about 1 hour to set.

TO STORE
Store in an airtight container in the fridge. They will keep for 2–3 days.

FREEZING TIP
__To freeze__ Complete the recipe to the end of step 3. Open-freeze, and then wrap and freeze.
__To use__ Thaw for about 1 hour, and then complete the recipe.

Dainty Cupcakes

Preparation Time 15 minutes, plus drying • Cooking Time 15–20 minutes, plus cooling and setting • Makes 12 •
Per Cupcake 306 calories, 14g fat (8g saturated), 46g carbohydrates, 400mg sodium • Easy

¼ cup (½ stick) unsalted butter,
    softened
¾ cup plus 2 tablespoons superfine
    sugar
3 large eggs
1⅓ cups plus 1 tablespoon all-
    purpose flour, sifted
1¼ teaspoons baking powder
finely grated zest and juice of
    1 unwaxed lemon (see Cook's Tip
    on page 162)

FOR THE FROSTED FLOWERS
1 large egg white
6 edible flowers, such as violas
superfine sugar to dust

FOR THE TOPPING
2 cups confectioners' sugar, sifted
1 drop violet food coloring
2–3 tablespoons lemon juice,
    strained

1. Preheat the oven to 375°F. Line a 12-cup muffin pan with paper muffin liners.

2. Put the butter and superfine sugar into a bowl and cream together until pale, light, and fluffy. Add the eggs, one at a time, and beat together, folding 1 tablespoon flour into the mixture if it looks as if it is going to curdle. Fold in the flour, baking powder, lemon zest, and juice, and mix well.

3. Spoon the batter into the liners and bake for 15–20 minutes until pale golden, risen, and springy to the touch. Transfer to a wire rack to cool completely.

4. To make the frosted flowers, whisk the egg white in a clean bowl for 30 seconds or until frothy. Brush over the flower petals and put on a wire rack resting on a piece of wax paper. Dust heavily with superfine sugar, and then leave the flowers to dry.

5. To make the topping, put the confectioners' sugar into a bowl with the food coloring. Mix in the lemon juice to make a smooth dropping consistency. Spoon the icing onto the cakes, and then decorate with the frosted flowers. Stand the cakes upright on the wire rack and leave for about 1 hour to set.

TO STORE
Store in an airtight container. They will keep for 3–5 days.

FREEZING TIP
To freeze Complete the recipe to the end of step 3. Open-freeze, and then wrap and freeze.
To use Thaw for about 1 hour, and then complete the recipe.

TRY SOMETHING DIFFERENT
Ginger and Orange Cupcakes
Replace the lemon zest and juice with orange and add two pieces of drained and chopped preserved ginger. Omit the frosted flowers and make the icing with orange juice instead of lemon. Decorate with finely chopped preserved ginger.

Cherry Almond Cupcakes

Preparation Time 30 minutes • Cooking Time 25 minutes, plus cooling and setting • Makes 12 •
Per Cupcake 405 calories, 21g fat (11g saturated), 53g carbohydrates, 400mg sodium • Easy

¾ cup (1½ sticks) **unsalted butter, softened**

¾ cup plus 2 tablespoons **superfine sugar**

3 large **eggs**

1⅛ cups plus 4 teaspoons **all-purpose flour, sifted**

2 teaspoons **baking powder**

¾ cup plus 1 tablespoon **ground almonds (almond meal)**

1 teaspoon **almond extract**

3 ounces **candied cherries, finely chopped**

FOR THE TOPPING

1 tablespoon **custard powder**

½ cup **milk**

4 tablespoons **unsalted butter, softened**

2¼ cups **confectioners' sugar, sifted**

red sugar sprinkles

1. Preheat the oven to 375°F. Line a 12-cup muffin pan with paper muffin liners.

2. Using a hand mixer, beat the butter and superfine sugar in a bowl, or beat with a wooden spoon, until pale and creamy. Gradually beat in the eggs until just combined. Using a metal spoon, fold in the flour, baking powder, ground almonds, almond extract, and cherries until combined. Divide the batter equally between the paper liners.

3. Bake for 20 minutes or until golden and risen. Leave to cool in the pan for 5 minutes, and then transfer to a wire rack to cool completely.

4. For the topping, put the custard powder into a bowl and add a little of the milk to make a smooth paste. Put the remaining milk into a saucepan and bring just to a boil. Pour the hot milk onto the custard paste and stir. Return to the milk pan and heat gently for 1–2 minutes until it thickens. Remove from the heat, cover with dampened wax paper to prevent a skin from forming, and cool completely.

5. Put the custard into a bowl and, using a hand mixer, beat in the butter. Chill for 30 minutes.

6. Gradually beat the confectioners' sugar into the chilled custard mixture until you have a smooth, thick frosting. Using a small spatula, spread a little custard cream over the top of each cake, and then decorate with sugar sprinkles. Stand the cakes upright on a wire rack and leave for about 1 hour to set.

TO STORE
Store in an airtight container in the fridge. They will keep for 2–3 days.

FREEZING TIP
To freeze Complete the recipe to the end of step 3. Open-freeze, and then wrap and freeze.
To use Thaw for about 1 hour, and then complete the recipe.

Apple Crumble Cupcakes

Preparation Time 20 minutes • Cooking Time 25 minutes, plus cooling • Makes 12 • Per Cupcake 215 calories, 10g fat (6g saturated), 31g carbohydrates, 200mg sodium • Easy

2 Pippin apples, cored
juice of 1 lemon
1½ cups plus 2 tablespoons all-purpose flour, sifted
2½ teaspoons baking powder
1 teaspoon ground cinnamon
½ cup plus 2 tablespoons packed light brown sugar
2 large eggs
7 tablespoons unsalted butter, melted

FOR THE CRUMBLE
⅓ cup all-purpose flour
2 tablespoons unsalted butter, chilled and cut into cubes
1½ tablespoons packed light brown sugar

1. Preheat the oven to 350°F. Line a 12-cup muffin pan with paper muffin liners.

2. Make the crumble. Put the flour into a bowl and, using your fingertips, rub in the butter until it resembles coarse bread crumbs. Stir in the sugar and set aside.

3. Coarsely grate the apples into a large bowl and mix in the lemon juice. Add the flour, baking powder, cinnamon, and sugar. Put the eggs and melted butter into a bowl and lightly beat together. Pour into the flour mixture. Stir with a spatula until just combined. Divide the batter equally between the paper liners. Then sprinkle the crumble equally over the top of each cake.

4. Bake for 25 minutes or until lightly golden and risen. Leave to cool in the pan for 5 minutes, and then transfer to a wire rack to cool completely.

TO STORE
Store in an airtight container. They will keep for 3–5 days.

FREEZING TIP
To freeze *Complete the recipe. Open-freeze, and then wrap and freeze.*
To use *Thaw for about 1 hour, then serve.*

Island Tropic Cupcakes

Preparation Time 40 minutes • Cooking Time 20 minutes, plus cooling and setting • Makes 12 •
Per Cupcake 287 calories, 6g fat (4g saturated), 61g carbohydrates, 100mg sodium • Easy

1 pink grapefruit

2 ounces dried cranberries

2 cups all-purpose flour, sifted

2¾ teaspoons baking powder

½ cup plus 2 tablespoons superfine
sugar

⅛ cup plus 1 tablespoon milk

1 large egg, beaten

6 tablespoons unsalted butter,
melted

FOR THE TOPPING

2⅔ cups fondant sugar, sifted

2–4 tablespoons water

red and yellow food coloring

⅛ cup apricot glaze (see Cook's Tip)

edible silver balls

cocktail umbrellas (optional)

1. Preheat the oven to 375°F. Line a 12-cup muffin pan with paper muffin liners.

2. Grate the zest from half the grapefruit into a bowl. Set aside. Cut the top and bottom off the grapefruit and stand it upright on a board. Using a serrated knife, cut away the pith in a downward motion. Cut in between the membranes to remove the segments. Process the segments in a food processor until pureed.

3. Transfer the puree into the bowl with the zest. Add the cranberries, flour, baking powder, superfine sugar, milk, egg, and melted butter and stir with a spatula until just combined. Divide the batter equally between the paper liners.

4. Bake for 20 minutes or until golden and risen. Leave to cool in the pan for 5 minutes, and then transfer to a wire rack to cool completely.

5. For the icing, put the fondant sugar into a bowl and add enough water (2–4 tablespoons) to make a smooth icing. Add a few drops of food coloring to make it pinky-orange in color. Brush the tops of the cakes with the apricot glaze, and then spoon a little icing onto each cake to flood the top. Decorate with the silver balls.

6. Stand the cakes upright on the wire rack and leave for about 1 hour to set. Decorate with a cocktail umbrella once set, if desired.

TO STORE

Store in an airtight container. They will keep for 3–5 days.

FREEZING TIP

To freeze Complete the recipe to the end of step 4. Open-freeze, and then wrap and freeze.

To use Thaw for about 1 hour, and then complete the recipe.

COOK'S TIP

Apricot Glaze

To make 18 ounces, you will need:
- *1 (18-ounce) jar apricot jam*
- *2 tablespoons water*

Put the jam and water into a pot and heat gently, stirring occasionally, until melted. Boil the jam rapidly for a minute, then strain through a strainer. Using a wooden spoon, rub through as much fruit as possible. Discard the skin left in the strainer.

Pour the glaze into a clean, hot jar, then seal with a clean lid and cool. Store in the refrigerator and warm very gently before using. It will keep for up to two months.

Meringue Cupcakes

Preparation Time 30 minutes • Cooking Time 25 minutes, plus cooling and setting • Makes 12 •
Per Cupcake 226 calories, 10g fat (6g saturated), 34g carbohydrates, 200mg sodium • Easy

½ cup (1 stick) unsalted butter,
   softened
½ cup superfine sugar
2 large eggs
1⅛ cups plus 4 teaspoons all-
   purpose flour, sifted
1 tablespoon milk
zest of 1 unwaxed lemon (see
   Cook's Tip on page 162)
⅓ cup small fresh blueberries
12 fresh raspberries

FOR THE TOPPING
1 large egg white
¾ cup plus 2 tablespoons superfine
   sugar
2 tablespoons water
a pinch of cream of tartar

1. Preheat the oven to 375°F. Line a 12-cup muffin pan with paper muffin liners.

2. Using a hand mixer, beat the butter and sugar in a bowl, or beat with a wooden spoon, until pale and creamy. Gradually beat in the eggs until just combined. Using a metal spoon, fold in the flour, milk, lemon zest, and blueberries until combined.

3. Divide the batter equally between the paper liners and press one raspberry into the center of each cake. Bake for 15 minutes or until golden and risen. Leave to cool in the pan for 5 minutes, and then transfer to a wire rack to cool completely.

4. For the frosting, put all the ingredients into a heatproof bowl and mix lightly using a hand mixer. Put the bowl over a pot of simmering water and whisk continuously for about 7 minutes or until the mixture thickens sufficiently to stand in peaks.

5. Insert a star tip into a pastry bag, and then fill the bag with the frosting and pipe a swirl onto the top of each cake. Stand the cakes upright on the wire rack and leave for about 1 hour to set.

TO STORE
Complete the recipe to the end of step 3. Store, un-iced, in an airtight container. They will keep for 3–5 days. Ice to serve.

FREEZING TIP
***To freeze** Complete the recipe to the end of step 3. Open-freeze, and then wrap and freeze.*
***To use** Thaw for about 1 hour, and then complete the recipe.*

Raspberry Cupcakes

Preparation Time 45 minutes • Cooking Time 2 hours 15–20 minutes (for the cakes), plus cooling • Makes 12 •
Per Cupcake 383 calories, 27g fat (17g saturated), 32g carbohydrates, 300mg sodium • A Little Effort

¾ cup (1½ sticks) unsalted butter,
    at room temperature
¾ cup plus 2 tablespoons superfine
    sugar
3 large eggs
1⅓ cups plus 1 tablespoon all-
    purpose flour, sifted
1¼ teaspoons baking powder
1 teaspoon vanilla extract
1 cup raspberries

FOR THE MERINGUES
1 large egg white
¼ cup superfine sugar
3–4 drops pink food coloring
2 tablespoons freeze-dried
    raspberries

FOR THE TOPPING
¾ cup raspberries
1¼ cups heavy cream
freeze-dried raspberries

1. Preheat the oven to 250°F. Line a baking sheet with parchment paper. Place the egg white in a medium bowl and whisk until stiff. Whisk 2 teaspoons of the sugar in and then fold in the remainder along with the food coloring.

2. Transfer the meringue to a pastry bag fitted with a large star tip and pipe 12 1¼-inch meringues onto the parchment paper. Sprinkle the top of each meringue with the freeze-dried raspberries. Bake the meringues for 2 hours. Place on a wire rack to cool completely.

3. Increase the oven temperature to 350°F. Line a 12-cup muffin pan with paper muffin liners. Using a hand mixer, beat the butter and superfine sugar in a bowl, or beat with a wooden spoon, until pale and creamy. Gradually beat in the eggs until just combined. Fold in the flour, baking powder, and vanilla, and stir well to combine. Carefully fold in the raspberries. Divide the batter evenly among the paper liners and bake for 15–20 minutes until pale golden and risen. Transfer to a wire rack to cool completely.

4. For the topping, whip the cream until soft peaks just form. Crush the raspberries with a fork and fold them gently into the whipped cream. Just before serving, place the raspberry cream into a pastry bag fitted with a large plain tip and pipe the cream on top of the cakes. Top each cake with a meringue and dust with the freeze-dried raspberries.

Chili Chocolate Cupcakes

Preparation Time 35 minutes • Cooking Time 15–20 minutes, plus cooling • Makes 12 •
Per Cupcake 367 calories, 26g fat (16g saturated), 32g carbohydrates, 400mg sodium • A Little Effort

¾ cup (1½ sticks) unsalted butter,
   at room temperature
¾ cup plus 2 tablespoons superfine
   sugar
3 large eggs
1⅓ cups plus 1 tablespoon all-
   purpose flour, sifted
1¼ teaspoons baking powder
¼ cup unsweetened cocoa powder,
   sifted
½ teaspoon red chili flakes (see
   Cook's Tip)
½ teaspoon ground cinnamon

FOR THE TOPPING
4 ounces semisweet chocolate with
   chili (at least 70% cocoa solids),
   broken into pieces
1 cup heavy cream
red chili flakes (optional)
12 small red chilies, to decorate
   (optional)

1. For the topping, place the chocolate and cream in a small heatproof bowl, over a pan of gently simmering water. Stir occasionally until the chocolate is melted. Put to one side to cool, until the mixture has thickened to a suitable consistency for piping.

2. Preheat the oven to 350°F. Line a 12-cup muffin pan with paper muffin liners. Using a hand mixer, beat the butter and superfine sugar in a bowl, or beat with a wooden spoon, until pale and creamy. Gradually beat in the eggs until just combined. Fold in the flour, baking powder, cocoa powder, chili flakes, and cinnamon and stir well to combine. Divide the batter evenly among the paper liners and bake for 15–20 minutes until risen. Transfer to a wire rack to cool completely.

3. Divide the chocolate topping between each cake and swirl using a small frosting spatula or the back of a teaspoon. Decorate with chili flakes and chilies, if desired.

COOK'S TIP
If red chili flakes are too spicy, look for Turkish red pepper flakes—they are less fiery than regular chili flakes.

Pistachio, Cardamom, and Rose Water Cupcakes

Preparation Time 35 minutes • Cooking Time 15–20 minutes, plus cooling • Makes 12 •
Per Cupcake 443 calories, 28g fat (15g saturated), 48g carbohydrates, 300mg sodium • Easy

¾ cup (1½ sticks) unsalted butter,
  at room temperature
¾ cup plus 2 tablespoons superfine
  sugar
3 large eggs
1 cup all-purpose flour, sifted
1 teaspoon baking powder
½ cup ground almonds (almond
  meal)
⅛ cup plus 2 teaspoons pistachio
  nuts, roughly chopped
6 cardamom pods, seeds removed
  and ground
1 teaspoon rose water

FOR THE TOPPING
½ cup (1 stick) unsalted butter,
  at room temperature
2–3 tablespoons warm water
2½ cups confectioners' sugar,
  sifted
½ teaspoon rose water
1–2 drops pink food coloring
whole pistachio nuts, to decorate

1. Preheat the oven to 350°F. Line a 12-cup muffin pan with paper muffin liners. Using a hand mixer, beat the butter and superfine sugar in a bowl, or beat with a wooden spoon, until pale and creamy. Gradually beat in the eggs until just combined.

2. Fold in the flour, baking powder, ground almonds, pistachios, ground cardamom, and rose water, and stir well to combine. Divide the batter evenly among the paper liners and bake for 15–20 minutes until pale golden, risen, and springy to the touch. Transfer to a wire rack to cool completely.

3. For the topping, place the butter in a bowl and cream until soft. Gradually beat the confectioners' sugar plus the warm water into the butter until smooth. Mix in the rose water and food coloring. Transfer the icing to a pastry bag with a star tip and pipe a swirl on top of each cupcake. Top each cupcake with a pistachio.

Chocolate Chestnut Cupcakes

Preparation Time 30 minutes • Cooking Time 20–25 minutes, plus cooling • Makes 12 •
Per Cupcake 255 calories, 18g fat (8g saturated), 21g carbohydrates, 100mg sodium • Easy • Gluten-free

3 large eggs

½ cup packed soft brown sugar

7 ounces canned chestnut purée

1 cup plus 2 tablespoons ground almonds (almond meal)

½ teaspoon baking powder

FOR THE TOPPING

4 ounces semisweet chocolate (at least 70% cocoa solids), broken into pieces

¾ cup heavy cream

1. Preheat the oven to 350°F. Line a 12-cup muffin pan with paper muffin liners.

2. For the topping, place the chocolate and cream in a small heatproof bowl, over a pan of gently simmering water. Stir occasionally until the chocolate is melted. Put to one side to cool, until the mixture has thickened to a suitable consistency for piping.

3. Using a hand mixer, beat the eggs and sugar in a medium mixing bowl until foamy.

4. Place the chestnut purée in a large mixing bowl and stir with a fork to soften. Gradually beat in the egg mixture, and then fold in the ground almonds and baking powder. Divide the batter evenly among the paper liners and bake for 20–25 minutes until just firm. Transfer to a wire rack to cool completely.

5. Transfer the chocolate mixture to a pastry bag fitted with a medium star tip and pipe small stars all over the top of each cake.

Cappuccino Cupcakes

Preparation Time 30 minutes • Cooking Time 15–20 minutes, plus cooling • Makes 12 •
Per Cupcake 369 calories, 17g fat (10g saturated), 53g carbohydrates, 300mg sodium • Easy

¾ cup (1½ sticks) unsalted butter,
    at room temperature
¾ cup plus 2 tablespoons superfine
    sugar
3 large eggs
1⅓ cups plus 1 tablespoon all-
    purpose flour, sifted
1¼ teaspoons baking powder
1 tablespoon unsweetened cocoa
    powder, sifted
3 tablespoons strong cold coffee

FOR THE TOPPING
1 teaspoon instant coffee granules
1 tablespoon boiling water
⅓ cup cream cheese
2⅔ cups confectioners' sugar,
    sifted
3 tablespoons finely grated
    semisweet chocolate (at least
    70% cocoa solids)
12 chocolate-coated coffee beans

1. Preheat the oven to 350°F. Line a 12-cup muffin pan with paper muffin liners.

2. Using a hand mixer, beat the butter and superfine sugar in a bowl, or beat with a wooden spoon, until pale and creamy. Gradually beat in the eggs until just combined.

3. Fold in the flour, baking powder, cocoa powder, and coffee and stir well to combine. Divide the batter evenly among the paper liners and bake for 15–20 minutes until risen and springy to the touch. Transfer to a wire rack to cool completely.

4. For the topping, stir the coffee into the boiling water until dissolved. Place the cream cheese in a medium bowl and stir with a fork to soften. Add the coffee mixture and beat until well combined. Gradually add the confectioners' sugar, stirring well until incorporated. Transfer to a pastry bag fitted with a medium plain tip.

5. Pipe a swirl of coffee cream onto the top of each cake. Sprinkle plenty of grated chocolate over the cream and decorate with a chocolate-coated coffee bean.

Key Lime Pie Cupcakes

Preparation Time 35 minutes • Cooking Time 15–20 minutes, plus cooling • Makes 12 •
Per Cupcake 294 calories, 14g fat (8g saturated), 41g carbohydrates, 300mg sodium • A Little Effort

¾ cup (1½ sticks) unsalted butter,
   at room temperature
¾ cup plus 2 tablespoons superfine
   sugar
3 large eggs
1⅓ cups plus 1 tablespoon all-
   purpose flour, sifted
1¼ teaspoons baking powder
zest and juice of 1 unwaxed lime
   (see Cook's Tip on page 162)

**FOR THE FILLING AND
TOPPING**
½ cup superfine sugar
3 tablespoons water
4 tablespoons lime curd
2 large egg whites
grated zest of 1 unwaxed lime

1. Preheat the oven to 350°F. Line a 12-cup muffin pan with paper muffin liners. Using a hand mixer, beat the butter and superfine sugar in a bowl, or beat with a wooden spoon, until pale and creamy. Gradually beat in the eggs until just combined.

2. Fold in the flour, baking powder, lime zest, and juice and stir well to combine. Divide the batter evenly among the paper liners and bake for 15–20 minutes until pale golden, risen, and springy to the touch. Transfer to a wire rack to cool completely.

3. For the topping, place the sugar in a small pan with the water over medium heat and stir until the sugar has dissolved. Set aside to cool.

4. Using a cake plunger or a teaspoon, carefully remove a small piece of sponge from the center of each cake. Crumble the sponge into a small mixing bowl and stir in the lime curd. Place the lime sponge mixture back into the center of each cake.

5. Using a hand mixer, whisk the egg whites in a medium mixing bowl until soft peaks form and they have doubled in volume. Keep whisking and gradually add the sugar syrup, until the meringue is glossy and thick.

6. Transfer the meringue to a pastry bag fitted with a plain tip and pipe a swirl over each cake. Carefully (taking care that the cases don't burn) brown the top of each cake using a cook's blowtorch until the meringue is golden. Decorate with the lime zest.

CANDY STORE SURPRISES

Be Mine Cupcakes

Preparation Time 30 minutes • Cooking Time 15 minutes, plus cooling • Makes 12 • Per Cupcake 289 calories, 15g fat (9g saturated), 40g carbohydrates, 300mg sodium • Easy

½ cup (1 stick) unsalted butter, softened

½ cup superfine sugar

2 large eggs

1 cup all-purpose flour, sifted

1½ teaspoons baking powder

2 ounces Turkish Delight candy, finely chopped

1 tablespoon rose water

FOR THE TOPPING

6 tablespoons unsalted butter, softened

2¼ cups confectioners' sugar, sifted

2 tablespoons rose water

pink and white heart-shaped sugar sprinkles

about 12 heart-shaped candies

1. Preheat the oven to 375°F. Line a 12-cup muffin pan with paper muffin liners.

2. Using a hand mixer, beat the butter and superfine sugar in a bowl, or beat with a wooden spoon, until pale and creamy. Gradually beat in the eggs until just combined. Using a metal spoon, fold in the flour, baking powder, Turkish Delight, and rose water until combined. Divide the batter equally between the paper liners.

3. Bake for 15 minutes or until golden and risen. Leave to cool in the pan for 5 minutes, and then transfer to a wire rack to cool completely.

4. For the topping, put the butter into a bowl and beat until fluffy. Add the confectioners' sugar and rose water, and beat until light and fluffy. Using a small spatula, spread a little buttercream over the top of each cake. Decorate with sugar hearts and top each with a heart-shaped candy.

TO STORE
Store in an airtight container. They will keep for 3–5 days.

FREEZING TIP
To freeze *Complete the recipe to the end of step 3. Open-freeze, and then wrap and freeze.*
To use *Thaw for about 1 hour, and then complete the recipe.*

Candy Shop Cupcakes

Preparation Time 30 minutes • Cooking Time 20 minutes, plus cooling and setting • Makes 12 •
Per Cupcake 424 calories, 19g fat (12g saturated), 64g carbohydrates, 600mg sodium • Easy

**¾ cup (1½ sticks) unsalted butter,
  softened**
**¾ cup plus 2 tablespoons superfine
  sugar**
3 large eggs
**1⅓ cups plus 1 tablespoon all-
  purpose flour, sifted**
**zest of 1 unwaxed lemon (see
  Cook's Tip on page 162)**
1¾ teaspoons baking powder
⅓ cup plus 2 teaspoons lemon curd

FOR THE TOPPING
**6 tablespoons unsalted butter,
  softened**
3 cups confectioners' sugar, sifted
¼ cup milk
**soft candies, jelly beans, or
  chocolate buttons**

1. Preheat the oven to 375°F. Line a 12-cup muffin pan with paper muffin liners.

2. Using a hand mixer, beat the butter and superfine sugar in a bowl, or beat with a wooden spoon, until pale and creamy. Gradually beat in the eggs until just combined. Using a metal spoon, fold in the flour, lemon zest, and baking powder until combined. Divide the batter equally between the paper liners.

3. Bake for 20 minutes or until golden and risen. Leave to cool in the pan for 5 minutes, and then transfer to a wire rack to cool completely.

4. Cut a small cone shape from the top of each cake. Put a teaspoonful of lemon curd into the hole in each cake and then replace the cake cone, pressing down lightly.

5. For the topping, put the butter into a bowl and beat until fluffy. Gradually add half the confectioners' sugar, mixing until combined. Add the milk and remaining confectioners' sugar, and beat until light and fluffy. Using a small spatula, spread a little frosting over each cake. Stand the cakes upright on a wire rack and leave for about 30 minutes to set. Decorate each cake with the candies when set.

TO STORE
Store in an airtight container. They will keep for 2–3 days.

FREEZING TIP
To freeze *Complete the recipe to the end of step 3. Open-freeze, and then wrap and freeze.*
To use *Thaw for about 1 hour, and then complete the recipe.*

Lemon Sorbet Cupcakes

Preparation Time 35 minutes • Cooking Time 15–20 minutes, plus cooling • Makes 12 •
Per Cupcake 244 calories, 14g fat (8g saturated), 29g carbohydrates, 300mg sodium • A Little Effort

¾ cup (1½ sticks) unsalted butter,
   at room temperature
¾ cup plus 2 tablespoons superfine
   sugar
3 large eggs
1⅓ cups plus 1 tablespoon all-
   purpose flour, sifted
1¼ teaspoons baking powder
zest and juice of 1 unwaxed lemon
   (see Cook's Tip on page 162)

FOR THE FILLING
3½ ounces lemon sorbet
12 edible sugared lemon seeds

1. Preheat the oven to 350°F. Line a baking sheet with parchment paper. Line a 12-cup muffin pan with paper muffin liners.

2. Using a melon baller or a teaspoon, scoop 12 balls of lemon sorbet. Place the balls on the lined baking sheet and place in the freezer until ready to serve.

3. Using a hand mixer, beat the butter and superfine sugar in a bowl, or beat with a wooden spoon, until pale and creamy. Gradually beat in the eggs until just combined.

4. Fold in the flour, baking powder, lemon zest, and juice and stir well to combine. Divide the batter evenly among the paper liners and bake for 15–20 minutes until pale golden, risen, and springy to the touch. Transfer to a wire rack to cool completely.

5. Using a cake plunger or a teaspoon, carefully remove a small piece of sponge from the center of each cake.

6. Just before serving, pop a ball of sorbet into the cutout hole in the center of each cake and top with a lemon seed. Serve immediately.

Candy Corn Cupcakes

Preparation Time 40 minutes • Cooking Time 15–20 minutes, plus cooling • Makes 12 •
Per Cupcake 422 calories, 24g fat (15g saturated), 51g carbohydrates, 300mg sodium • Easy

¾ cup (1½ sticks) unsalted butter,
    at room temperature
¾ cup plus 2 tablespoons superfine
    sugar
3 large eggs
1⅓ cups plus 1 tablespoon all-
    purpose flour, sifted
1¼ teaspoons baking powder
1 teaspoon vanilla extract
finely grated zest of 1 unwaxed
    orange (see Cook's Tip on
    page 162)

FOR THE TOPPING
½ cup (1 stick) unsalted butter,
    at room temperature
2½ cups confectioners' sugar,
    sifted
2–3 tablespoons warm water
candy corn candies, to decorate

1. Preheat the oven to 350°F. Line a 12-cup muffin pan with paper muffin liners.

2. Using a hand mixer, beat the butter and superfine sugar in a bowl, or beat with a wooden spoon, until pale and creamy. Gradually beat in the eggs until just combined. Fold in the flour, baking powder, and vanilla, and stir well to combine. Stir in the orange zest until thoroughly mixed. Divide the batter evenly among the paper liners and bake for 15–20 minutes until pale golden, risen, and springy to the touch. Transfer to a wire rack to cool completely.

3. For the topping, place the butter in a bowl and cream until soft. Gradually beat the confectioners' sugar plus the warm water into the butter until smooth.

4. Transfer the frosting to a pastry bag fitted with a star tip and pipe a swirl of frosting on each cupcake. Top each cake with a candy corn.

Peanut Butter Cupcakes

Preparation Time 30 minutes • Cooking Time 15–20 minutes, plus cooling • Makes 12 •
Per Cupcake 659 calories, 33g fat (16g saturated), 88g carbohydrates, 600mg sodium • Easy

¾ cup (1½ sticks) unsalted butter,
   at room temperature
¾ cup plus 2 tablespoons superfine
   sugar
3 large eggs
1⅓ cups plus 1 tablespoon all-
   purpose flour, sifted
1¼ teaspoons baking powder
4 tablespoons creamy peanut
   butter

FOR THE TOPPING
⅔ cup cream cheese
5¼ cups confectioners' sugar,
   sifted
1 tablespoon warm water
6 tablespoons creamy peanut
   butter
12 mini peanut butter cups, halved
3 ounces peanut butter candies

1. Preheat the oven to 350°F. Line a 12-cup muffin pan with paper muffin liners. Using a hand mixer, beat the butter and superfine sugar in a bowl, or beat with a wooden spoon, until pale and creamy. Gradually beat in the eggs until just combined.

2. Fold in the flour, baking powder, and peanut butter, and stir well to combine. Divide the batter evenly among the paper liners and bake for 15–20 minutes until risen and springy to the touch. Transfer to a wire rack to cool completely.

3. For the topping, place the cream cheese in a medium bowl and stir with a fork to soften. Gradually add the sifted confectioners' sugar plus the warm water, stirring well until incorporated. Stir in the peanut butter.

4. Transfer the frosting to a pastry bag fitted with a large star tip. Pipe swirls of frosting over the cakes and top each cake with half a mini peanut butter cup and five peanut butter candies.

Chocolate and Coconut Cupcakes

Preparation Time 35 minutes • Cooking Time 15–20 minutes, plus cooling • Makes 12 •
Per Cupcake 590 calories, 36g fat (24g saturated), 66g carbohydrates, 300mg sodium • A Little Effort

¾ cup (1½ sticks) salted butter, at
   room temperature
¾ cup plus 2 tablespoons superfine
   sugar
3 large eggs
1 cup all-purpose flour, sifted
1 teaspoon baking powder
2 tablespoons unsweetened cocoa
   powder, sifted
¾ cup dry unsweetened coconut
2 ounces white chocolate chunks

FOR THE TOPPING
3 tablespoons dry unsweetened
   coconut
1 cup (2 sticks) unsalted butter,
   at room temperature
4 cups confectioners' sugar, sifted
2 tablespoons unsweetened cocoa
   powder, sifted
2–3 tablespoons warm water
mini white chocolate stars, to
   decorate

1. Preheat the oven to 350°F. Line a 12-cup muffin pan with paper muffin liners. Using a hand mixer, beat the butter and superfine sugar in a bowl, or beat with a wooden spoon, until pale and creamy. Gradually beat in the eggs until just combined.

2. Fold in the flour, baking powder, cocoa powder, and coconut, and stir well to combine. Fold in the white chocolate chunks. Divide the batter evenly among the paper liners and bake for 15–20 minutes until risen and springy to the touch. Transfer to a wire rack to cool completely.

3. For the topping, heat a small nonstick skillet over high heat. Add the unsweetened coconut and toast until browned, give the pan a shake occasionally to prevent it from burning. Set aside.

4. Place the butter in a bowl and cream until soft. Gradually beat the confectioners' sugar, cocoa powder, and the warm water into the butter until smooth.

5. Transfer the frosting to a pastry bag fitted with a large star tip and pipe a swirl of frosting over each cake. Arrange the chocolate stars all over the frosting and sprinkle a little toasted coconut over each cupcake.

Marshmallow Madness Cupcakes

Preparation Time 40 minutes • Cooking Time 20–25 minutes, plus cooling and setting • Makes 12 •
Per Cupcake 317 calories, 13g fat (2g saturated), 49g carbohydrates, 100mg sodium • Easy

3 large eggs
1⅓ cups plus 1 tablespoon all-
purpose flour, sifted
¾ cup superfine sugar
¾ cup sunflower oil
1¾ teaspoons baking powder
¼ cup plus 1 teaspoon white
chocolate chips

FOR THE TOPPING
4 ounces pink and white
marshmallows
1 large egg white
¾ cup superfine sugar
a pinch of cream of tartar
pink sugar sprinkles

1. Preheat the oven to 375°F. Line a 12-cup muffin pan with paper muffin liners.

2. Put the eggs, flour, sugar, oil, and baking powder into a large bowl and, using a hand mixer, beat until just combined. Add the chocolate chips and fold through. Divide the batter equally between the paper liners.

3. Bake for 20–25 minutes until lightly golden and risen. Leave to cool in the pan for 5 minutes, and then transfer to a wire rack to cool completely.

4. For the topping, reserve six white marshmallows. Put the remaining marshmallows, the egg white, sugar, and a pinch of cream of tartar into a heatproof bowl, and beat lightly using a hand mixer. Put the bowl over a pot of simmering water and whisk continuously for about 7 minutes or until the marshmallows have melted and the mixture thickens sufficiently to stand in peaks.

5. Cut the reserved marshmallows in half. Spread a little of the icing over the top of each cake. Scatter with sugar sprinkles and top each with a marshmallow half. Stand the cakes upright on the wire rack and leave for about 1 hour to set.

TO STORE
Store in an airtight container. They will keep for 3–5 days.

FREEZING TIP
__To freeze__ Complete the recipe to the end of step 3. Open-freeze, and then wrap and freeze.
__To use__ Thaw for about 1 hour, and then complete the recipe.

Rocky Road Cupcakes

Preparation Time 30 minutes • Cooking Time 15–20 minutes, plus cooling and setting • Makes 9 •
Per Cupcake 360 calories, 20g fat (11g saturated), 45g carbohydrates, 500mg sodium • Easy

7 tablespoons unsalted butter,
    softened
½ cup plus 2 tablespoons superfine
    sugar
2 large eggs
1⅛ cups plus 4 teaspoons all-
    purpose flour, sifted
1 teaspoon baking powder
1 ounce candied cherries, diced
⅛ cup plus 1 teaspoon milk
    chocolate chips
¼ cup pine nuts

FOR THE TOPPING
3½ ounces milk chocolate
¼ cup heavy cream
½ cup mini marshmallows
1 ounce candied cherries, finely
    chopped
2¼ ounces malted milk balls

1. Preheat the oven to 375°F. Line a 12-cup muffin pan with nine paper muffin liners.

2. Using a hand mixer, beat the butter and sugar in a bowl, or beat with a wooden spoon, until pale and creamy. Gradually beat in the eggs until just combined. Using a metal spoon, fold in the flour, baking powder, cherries, chocolate chips, and pine nuts until combined. Divide the batter equally between the paper liners.

3. Bake for 15–20 minutes until golden and risen. Leave to cool in the pan for 5 minutes, and then transfer to a wire rack to cool completely.

4. For the topping, break the chocolate into pieces, and then put into a heatproof bowl with the cream. Set over a pan of gently simmering water, making sure the bottom of the bowl doesn't touch the water. Heat until melted, stirring occasionally until smooth.

5. Remove from the heat and, using a small spatula, spread a little over the top of each cake. Decorate each cake with marshmallows, cherries, and the malted milk balls. Stand the cakes upright on the wire rack and leave for about 1 hour to set.

TO STORE
Store in an airtight container in the fridge. They will keep for 2–3 days.

FREEZING TIP
To freeze *Complete the recipe to the end of step 3. Open-freeze, and then wrap and freeze.*
To use *Thaw for about 1 hour, and then complete the recipe.*

Coffee Walnut Cupcakes

Preparation Time 30 minutes • Cooking Time 20–25 minutes, plus cooling and chilling • Makes 12 •
Per Cupcake 409 calories, 26g fat (11g saturated), 43g carbohydrates, 500mg sodium • Easy

1 cup walnuts
¾ cup (1½ sticks) unsalted butter, softened
1⅛ cups plus 4 teaspoons all-purpose flour, sifted
¾ cup plus 2 tablespoons packed light brown sugar
3 large eggs
2 teaspoons baking powder
⅛ cup plus 1 tablespoon milk

FOR THE TOPPING

2 tablespoons boiling water
1 tablespoon instant coffee granules
4 tablespoons unsalted butter, softened
1¾ cups confectioners' sugar, sifted
½ cup walnuts, finely chopped

1. Preheat the oven to 375°F. Line a 12-cup muffin pan with paper muffin liners.

2. Whiz the walnuts in a food processor until finely ground. Transfer to a large bowl and add the remaining ingredients. Using a hand mixer, beat together until pale and creamy. Divide the batter equally between the paper liners.

3. Bake for 20–25 minutes until golden and risen. Leave to cool in the pan for 5 minutes, and then transfer to a wire rack to cool completely.

4. For the topping, put the boiling water into a small bowl, add the coffee, and stir to dissolve. Put the butter, ¾ cup of the confectioners' sugar, and the coffee mixture into a bowl, and beat until combined. Chill for 30 minutes.

5. Remove the buttercream from the fridge and gradually mix in the remaining confectioners' sugar until smooth and fluffy. Using a small spatula, spread a little buttercream over the top of each cake. Put the chopped walnuts into a shallow bowl and lightly dip the top of each cake into the walnuts.

TO STORE
Store in an airtight container. They will keep for 2–3 days.

FREEZING TIP
To freeze Complete the recipe to the end of step 3. Open-freeze, and then wrap and freeze.
To use Thaw for about 1 hour, and then complete the recipe.

Cookies and Cream Cupcakes

Preparation Time 30 minutes • Cooking Time 15–20 minutes, plus cooling • Makes 12 •
Per Cupcake 357 calories, 21g fat (13g saturated), 41g carbohydrates, 500mg sodium • Easy

3 ounces mini chocolate sandwich cookies

¾ cup (1½ sticks) unsalted butter, softened

¾ cup superfine sugar

3 large eggs

1⅓ cups plus 1 tablespoon all-purpose flour, sifted

1¾ teaspoons baking powder

3 tablespoons milk

½ teaspoon vanilla extract

FOR THE TOPPING

6 tablespoons unsalted butter, softened

1⅓ cups confectioners' sugar, sifted

2 teaspoons vanilla extract

1 teaspoon unsweetened cocoa powder

1. Preheat the oven to 400°F. Line a 12-cup muffin pan with paper muffin liners. Reserve 12 mini cookies and roughly chop the remainder.

2. Using a hand mixer, beat the butter and superfine sugar in a bowl, or beat with a wooden spoon, until pale and creamy. Gradually beat in the eggs until just combined. Using a metal spoon, fold in the flour, baking powder, milk, vanilla extract, and chopped cookies until combined. Divide the batter equally between the paper liners.

3. Bake for 15–20 minutes until golden and risen. Leave to cool in the pan for 5 minutes, and then transfer to a wire rack to cool completely.

4. For the topping, put the butter into a bowl and beat until fluffy. Gradually add the confectioners' sugar and vanilla extract, and beat until light and fluffy. Using a small spatula, spread the buttercream over the top of each cake. Sift a little cocoa powder over the buttercream, and then decorate each with a reserved cookie.

TO STORE

Store in an airtight container. They will keep for 2–3 days.

FREEZING TIP

__To freeze__ Complete the recipe to the end of step 3. Open-freeze, and then wrap and freeze.
__To use__ Thaw for about 1 hour, and then complete the recipe.

Pastis Cupcakes

Preparation Time 30 minutes • Cooking Time 20–25 minutes, plus cooling • Makes 12 • Per Cupcake 291 calories, 15g fat (9g saturated), 37g carbohydrates, 400mg sodium • Easy

½ cup (1 stick) unsalted butter, softened

1 cup superfine sugar

2 large eggs

1½ cups plus 2 tablespoons all-purpose flour, sifted

1½ teaspoons baking powder

1 ounce custard powder

2 tablespoons caraway seeds

½ cup milk

FOR THE TOPPING

6 tablespoons unsalted butter, softened

2⅔ cups confectioners' sugar, sifted

2 tablespoons Pernod*

1 tablespoon boiling water

pale blue sugar sprinkles

1. Preheat the oven to 375°F. Line a 12-cup muffin pan with paper muffin liners.

2. Using a hand mixer, beat the butter and superfine sugar in a bowl, or beat with a wooden spoon, until pale and creamy. Gradually beat in the eggs until just combined. Using a metal spoon, fold in the flour, baking powder, custard powder, caraway seeds, and milk until combined. Divide the batter equally between the paper liners.

3. Bake for 20–25 minutes until golden and risen. Leave to cool in the pan for 5 minutes, and then transfer to a wire rack to cool completely.

4. For the topping, put the butter into a bowl and beat until fluffy. Gradually beat in half the confectioners' sugar. Then add the Pernod, the boiling water, and the remaining confectioners' sugar, and beat until light and fluffy. Using a small spatula, spread a little of the frosting over the top of each cake, and then sprinkle with the blue sugar sprinkles.

* This recipe is not suitable for children because it contains alcohol.

TO STORE
Store in an airtight container. They will keep for 3–5 days.

FREEZING TIP
To freeze *Complete the recipe to the end of step 3. Open-freeze, and then wrap and freeze.*
To use *Thaw for about 1 hour, and then complete the recipe.*

Honeycomb Cream Cupcakes

Preparation Time 30 minutes • Cooking Time 20 minutes, plus cooling • Makes 9 • Per Cupcake 480 calories, 25g fat (15g saturated), 65g carbohydrates, 600mg sodium • Easy

½ cup (1 stick) unsalted butter, softened

¼ cup superfine sugar

2 large eggs

¼ cup plus 2 teaspoons honey

1 cup all-purpose flour

½ cup plus 2 teaspoons rolled oats

1½ teaspoons baking powder

1 tablespoon milk

FOR THE TOPPING

½ cup (1 stick) unsalted butter, softened

2⅔ cups confectioners' sugar, sifted

2 tablespoons milk

1 toffee candy bar, thinly sliced

1. Preheat the oven to 375°F. Line a 12-cup muffin pan with nine paper muffin liners.

2. Using a hand mixer, beat the butter and superfine sugar in a bowl, or beat with a wooden spoon, until pale and creamy. Gradually beat in the eggs and honey until just combined. Using a metal spoon, fold in the flour, oats, baking powder, and milk until combined. Divide the batter equally between the paper liners.

3. Bake for 20 minutes or until golden and risen. Leave to cool in the pan for 5 minutes, and then transfer to a wire rack to cool completely.

4. For the topping, put the butter into a bowl and beat until fluffy. Gradually beat in half the confectioners' sugar. Add the milk and the remaining confectioners' sugar, and beat until light and fluffy.

5. Insert a star tip into a pastry bag. Then fill the bag with the buttercream and pipe a swirl onto the top of each cake. When ready to serve, decorate each with slices of the toffee candy bar.

TO STORE
Store in an airtight container. They will keep for 2–3 days.

FREEZING TIP
To freeze Complete the recipe to the end of step 3. Open-freeze, and then wrap and freeze.
To use Thaw for about 1 hour, and then complete the recipe.

Truffle Kisses Cupcakes

Preparation Time 40 minutes • Cooking Time 30 minutes, plus cooling and setting • Makes 18 •
Per Cupcake 317 calories, 20g fat (10g saturated), 34g carbohydrates, 200mg sodium • Easy

⅔ cup (1⅓ sticks) **unsalted butter,**
   softened
1 cup **superfine sugar**
3 large **eggs**
1½ cups plus 2 tablespoons **all-**
   purpose flour, sifted
1 teaspoon **baking powder**
½ teaspoon **baking soda**
⅔ cup **roasted hazelnuts, chopped**
¾ cup plus 1 tablespoon **buttermilk**
½ ounce **semisweet chocolate,**
   finely grated

FOR THE TOPPING
¾ cup **heavy cream**
5 ounces **semisweet chocolate**
3½ ounces **milk chocolate, finely**
   chopped
18 small **chocolate truffles**
   (optional)

1. Preheat the oven to 350°F. Line a
12-cup and a 6-cup muffin pan with
paper muffin liners.

2. Using a hand mixer, beat the
butter and sugar in a bowl, or beat
with a wooden spoon, until pale and
creamy. Gradually beat in the eggs
until just combined. Using a metal
spoon, fold in the flour, the baking
powder, baking soda, hazelnuts,
buttermilk, and grated chocolate
until combined. Divide the batter
equally between the paper liners.

3. Bake for 20–25 minutes until
golden and risen. Leave to cool in
the pan for 5 minutes, and then
transfer to a wire rack to cool
completely.

4. For the topping, heat the cream
in a small saucepan until nearly
boiling. Finely chop 3½ ounces of
the semisweet chocolate and put
into a bowl along with all the milk
chocolate. Pour the hot cream over
the chocolate and leave to stand
for 5 minutes, and then stir gently
until smooth. Chill the mixture for
15–20 minutes until thickened
slightly.

5. Using a spatula, spread a
little chocolate cream over the top
of each cake. Finely grate the
remaining semisweet chocolate
over the top of each cake. Finish
each with a chocolate truffle, if
desired. Stand the cakes upright
on the wire rack and leave for about
1 hour to set.

TO STORE
*Store in an airtight container in the
fridge. They will keep for 2–3 days.*

FREEZING TIP
*To freeze Complete the recipe to
the end of step 3. Open-freeze, and
then wrap and freeze.*
*To use Thaw for about 1 hour, and
then complete the recipe.*

Marbled Chocolate Cupcakes

Preparation Time 40 minutes • Cooking Time 20 minutes, plus cooling • Makes 12 • Per Cupcake 360 calories, 16g fat (10g saturated), 54g carbohydrates, 500mg sodium • Easy

6 tablespoons unsalted butter, softened
¾ cup superfine sugar
2 large eggs
1 cup all-purpose flour, sifted
¼ teaspoon baking powder
½ teaspoon baking soda
2 teaspoons vanilla extract
⅔ cup buttermilk
¼ cup unsweetened cocoa powder, sifted

FOR THE TOPPING
½ cup (1 stick) unsalted butter, softened
3 cups confectioners' sugar, sifted
2 teaspoons vanilla extract
2 tablespoons boiling water
2 tablespoons unsweetened cocoa powder, sifted

1. Preheat the oven to 375°F. Line a 12-cup muffin pan with paper muffin liners.

2. Using a hand mixer, beat the butter and superfine sugar in a bowl, or beat with a wooden spoon, until pale and creamy. Gradually beat in the eggs until just combined. Using a metal spoon, fold in the flour, baking powder, baking soda, vanilla extract, and buttermilk until combined. Put half this mixture into another bowl and beat in the unsweetened cocoa powder. Very lightly fold this mixture into the vanilla mixture to create a marbled effect. Divide the batter equally between the paper liners.

3. Bake for 20 minutes or until golden and risen. Leave to cool in the pan for 5 minutes, and then transfer to a wire rack to cool completely.

4. For the topping, put the butter into a bowl and beat until fluffy. Gradually beat in half the confectioners' sugar. Then add the vanilla extract, the boiling water, and the remaining confectioners' sugar, and beat until light and fluffy. Put half the mixture into another bowl and beat in the unsweetened cocoa powder.

5. Insert a star tip into a pastry bag, and then fill the bag alternately with the vanilla and chocolate buttercreams. Pipe a swirl onto the top of each cake.

TO STORE
Store in an airtight container. They will keep for 3–5 days.

FREEZING TIP
To freeze *Complete the recipe to the end of step 3. Open-freeze, and then wrap and freeze.*
To use *Thaw for about 1 hour, and then complete the recipe.*

S'mores Cupcakes

Preparation Time 30 minutes • Cooking Time 15–20 minutes, plus cooling • Makes 12 •
Per Cupcake 270 calories, 14g fat (8g saturated), 35g carbohydrates, 300mg sodium • A Little Effort

¾ cup (1½ sticks) unsalted butter,
   at room temperature
¾ cup plus 2 tablespoons superfine
   sugar
3 large eggs
1⅓ cups plus 1 tablespoon all-
   purpose flour, sifted
1¼ teaspoons baking powder
1 teaspoon vanilla extract
2–3 drops pink food coloring
2 ounces milk chocolate chips

**FOR THE FILLING AND
   TOPPING**
½ cup superfine sugar
4 tablespoons water
2 large egg whites
2–3 drops pink food coloring
2 ounces white chocolate
2 graham crackers, crumbled
confectioners' sugar, for dusting

1. Preheat the oven to 350°F. Line a baking sheet with parchment paper. Line a 12-cup muffin pan with paper muffin liners. Using a hand mixer, beat the butter and superfine sugar in a bowl, or beat with a wooden spoon, until pale and creamy. Gradually beat in the eggs until just combined.

2. Fold in the flour, baking powder, vanilla, and coloring, and stir well to combine. Stir in the chocolate chips and mix thoroughly. Divide the batter evenly among the paper liners and bake for 15–20 minutes until risen and springy to the touch. Transfer to a wire rack to cool completely.

3. For the topping, place the sugar in a small pan with the water over medium heat and stir until the sugar has dissolved. Set aside to cool.

4. Using an electric mixer, whisk the egg whites until soft peaks form and they have doubled in volume. Keep whisking and gradually drizzle in the sugar syrup, until the meringue is glossy and thick. Add the food coloring and fold through until the meringue is a pale pink color.

5. Using a cake plunger or a teaspoon, carefully remove a small piece of sponge from the center of each cake. For the filling, break the white chocolate into pieces, and then put into a heatproof bowl. Set over a pan of gently simmering water, making sure the bottom of the bowl doesn't touch the water. Heat until melted, stirring occasionally until smooth. Spoon the melted white chocolate into the center of each cupcake. Sprinkle the graham crackers on top.

6. Either spoon the meringue over the cakes or transfer the meringue to a pastry bag fitted with a large star tip and pipe generous swirls of the mixture over the cakes. Carefully (taking care that the liners don't burn) brown the top of each cake using a cook's blowtorch until the meringue is browned. Dust the cakes with confectioners' sugar to serve.

Salted Caramel Cupcakes

Preparation Time 30 minutes • Cooking Time 15–20 minutes, plus cooling • Makes 12 •
Per Cupcake 613 calories, 33g fat (20g saturated), 80g carbohydrates, 300mg sodium • Easy

¾ cup (1½ sticks) salted butter,
   at room temperature
¾ cup plus 2 tablespoons superfine
   sugar
3 large eggs
1⅓ cups plus 1 tablespoon all-
   purpose flour, sifted
1¼ teaspoons baking powder
4 ounces semisweet chocolate with
   sea salt, finely chopped

FOR THE TOPPING
1 cup (2 sticks) unsalted butter,
   at room temperature
4 cups confectioners' sugar, sifted
½ (14-ounce) can caramel
coarse pink or white sea salt
   crystals, to decorate

1. Preheat the oven to 350°F. Line a 12-cup muffin pan with paper muffin liners.

2. Using a hand mixer, beat the butter and superfine sugar in a bowl, or beat with a wooden spoon, until pale and creamy. Gradually beat in the eggs until just combined.

3. Fold in the flour, baking powder, and chopped chocolate, and stir well to combine. Divide the batter evenly among the paper liners and bake for 15–20 minutes until risen and springy to the touch. Transfer to a wire rack to cool completely.

4. For the topping, place the butter in a bowl and cream until soft. Gradually beat the confectioners' sugar plus 6 tablespoons of the caramel into the butter until smooth. Divide the remaining caramel, apart from 2 tablespoons, between the cakes and spread it out using the back of a teaspoon.

5. Transfer the frosting to a large pastry bag fitted with a star tip and pipe swirls of frosting over each cake. Drizzle a little caramel and sprinkle a few flakes of salt over each cake.

Mint Chocolate Cupcakes

Preparation Time 35 minutes • Cooking Time 15–20 minutes, plus cooling • Makes 12 •
Per Cupcake 191 calories, 12g fat (7g saturated), 20g carbohydrates, 110mg sodium • Easy

½ cup (1 stick) unsalted butter, at
   room temperature
½ cup plus 2 tablespoons superfine
   sugar
2 large eggs
3 tablespoons milk
4 drops peppermint extract
¾ cup all-purpose flour
1¾ teaspoons baking powder
¼ cup unsweetened cocoa powder
2 ounces white chocolate chunks

FOR THE TOPPING
1½ ounces dark chocolate, broken
   into pieces
1½ ounces white chocolate, broken
   into pieces
¼ bunch fresh mint leaves

1. Preheat the oven to 350°F. Line a 12-cup muffin pan with paper muffin liners. Using a hand mixer, beat the butter and superfine sugar in a bowl, or beat with a wooden spoon, until pale and creamy. Gradually beat in the eggs until just combined. Stir in the milk and peppermint extract.

2. Fold in the flour, baking powder, and cocoa powder. Stir the chocolate chunks into the batter and divide it evenly among the paper liners. Bake for 10–15 minutes until risen and springy to the touch. Transfer to a wire rack to cool completely.

3. For the topping, melt the chocolates in separate heatproof bowls, over pans of simmering water. Let cool slightly then place them in separate pastry bags fitted with fine tips.

4. Drizzle the semisweet chocolate over the top of each cake in zigzag lines, and then drizzle the white chocolate in zigzag lines over the top in the opposite direction. Decorate each cake with a mint leaf.

Peanut Brittle Cupcakes

Preparation Time 35 minutes • Cooking Time 15–20 minutes, plus cooling • Makes 12 •
Per Cupcake 659 calories, 33g fat (16g saturated), 88g carbohydrates, 600mg sodium • Easy

¾ cup (1½ sticks) unsalted butter,
    at room temperature
¾ cup plus 2 tablespoons superfine
    sugar
3 large eggs
1⅓ cups plus 1 tablespoon all-
    purpose flour, sifted
1¼ teaspoons baking powder
4 tablespoons crunchy peanut
    butter

FOR THE TOPPING

1 cup (2 sticks) unsalted butter,
    at room temperature
4 cups confectioners' sugar, sifted
4 tablespoons smooth peanut butter
2 ounces peanut brittle, roughly
    chopped

1. Preheat the oven to 350°F. Line a 12-cup muffin pan with paper muffin liners. Using a hand mixer, beat the butter and superfine sugar in a bowl, or beat with a wooden spoon, until pale and creamy. Gradually beat in the eggs until just combined.

2. Fold in the flour, baking powder, and crunchy peanut butter, and stir well to combine. Divide the batter evenly among the paper liners and bake for 15–20 minutes until risen and springy to the touch. Transfer to a wire rack to cool completely.

3. For the topping, place the butter in a bowl and cream until soft. Gradually beat the confectioners' sugar and peanut butter into the butter until smooth.

4. Add 3 heaping tablespoons of the frosting onto each cake and, using a small spatula, work the frosting around into a cone shape. Top each cake with chopped peanut brittle.

SPECIAL OCCASION
CUPCAKES

New Year's Cupcakes

Preparation Time 35 minutes • Cooking Time 15–20 minutes, plus cooling • Makes 12 •
Per Cupcake 342 calories, 25g fat (15g saturated), 28g carbohydrates, 300mg sodium • Easy

¾ cup (1½ sticks) unsalted butter,
   at room temperature
¾ cup plus 2 tablespoons superfine
   sugar
3 large eggs
1⅓ cups plus 1 tablespoon all-
   purpose flour, sifted
1¼ teaspoons baking powder
1 teaspoon Champagne flavoring

FOR THE TOPPING
1 cup whipping or heavy cream
6 strawberries, halved
confectioners' sugar, for dusting

1. Preheat the oven to 350°F. Line a 12-cup muffin pan with paper muffin liners. Using a hand mixer, beat the butter and superfine sugar in a bowl, or beat with a wooden spoon, until pale and creamy. Gradually beat in the eggs until just combined.

2. Fold in the flour, baking powder, and champagne flavoring, and stir well to combine. Divide the batter evenly among the paper liners and bake for 15–20 minutes until pale golden, risen, and springy to the touch. Transfer to a wire rack to cool completely.

3. Whip the cream until soft peaks just form. Transfer to a pastry bag fitted with a medium star tip. Pipe large swirls of cream over each cupcake, top with half a strawberry, and dust with confectioners' sugar.

Super Bowl Cupcakes

Preparation Time 30 minutes • Cooking Time 15–20 minutes, plus cooling • Makes 12 •
Per Cupcake 393 calories, 14g fat (8g saturated), 38g carbohydrates, 300mg sodium • A Little Effort

¾ cup (1½ sticks) unsalted butter,
   at room temperature
¾ cup plus 2 tablespoons superfine
   sugar
3 large eggs
1⅓ cups plus 1 tablespoon all-
   purpose flour, sifted
1¼ teaspoons baking powder
1 teaspoon vanilla extract

FOR THE TOPPING
confectioners' sugar, for dusting
7 ounces green fondant icing
8 ounces brown fondant icing
3½ ounces white fondant icing
tools—number cutters

1. Preheat the oven to 350°F. Line a 12-cup muffin pan with paper muffin liners. Using a hand mixer, beat the butter and superfine sugar in a bowl, or beat with a wooden spoon, until pale and creamy. Gradually beat in the eggs until just combined.

2. Fold in the flour, baking powder, and vanilla, and stir well to combine. Divide the batter evenly among the paper liners and bake for 15–20 minutes until risen and springy to the touch. Transfer to a wire rack to cool completely.

3. On a counter lightly dusted with confectioners' sugar, roll out the green fondant icing to a thickness of ⅛ inch. Cut out 12 circles using a 3-inch plain cutter. Brush each circle with water and place on the top of each cake.

4. With the brown fondant icing shape 6 soccer balls and place white fondant icing on top to make the laces. Place 6 on top of the green fondant icing, attaching each one by sprinkling the bottom with a bit of water.

5. On a counter lightly dusted with confectioners' sugar, roll out the white fondant icing to a thickness of ⅛ inch. Cut out numbers as well as long strips to make the yard lines. Attach the yard lines and numbers with water to the top of 6 cupcakes.

Valentine Cupcakes

Preparation Time 30 minutes • Cooking Time 20 minutes, plus cooling • Makes 10 •
Per Cupcake 291 calories, 12g fat (3g saturated), 46g carbohydrates, 500mg sodium • Easy

1 cup all-purpose flour
½ cup plus 2 tablespoons superfine
   sugar
1½ teaspoons baking powder
½ cup (1 stick) soft margarine or
   butter, plus extra for greasing
2 extra-large eggs
1 teaspoon vanilla extract

FOR THE TOPPING
plain candied icing (see Cook's
   Tip)
food coloring of your choice
   (preferably gel)
edible glue
red edible glitter
metallic foil cupcake liners

1. Preheat the oven to 375°F. Carefully grease a 12-cup straight-sided silicone heart-shaped muffin tray.

2. Sift the flour, sugar, and baking powder into a bowl, food processor, or mixer. Add the margarine or butter, eggs, and vanilla, and beat until pale and creamy. Spoon the batter carefully into the muffin tray, place on a metal baking sheet, and bake for 20 minutes or until golden and firm to the touch. Leave to cool in the muffin tray, and then turn the cupcakes out onto a wire rack and leave to cool completely.

3. To create a level surface, slice the tops off the cupcakes and turn the cakes upside down (you will be icing the bottom of the cakes). Make the candied icing and tint it to your chosen color. Drizzle the icing all over the cakes and let it run down the sides.

4. Before the icing is completely dry, lay out all your metallic cupcake liners. Dip your fingers into a bowl of cold water, and then lift the cakes onto the liners (this keeps the icing from sticking to your fingers). Carefully mold the liners around the hearts.

5. When the icing is completely dry, paint the entire top with edible glue and dip into the glitter.

COOK'S TIP
Candied icing
• *2 cups confectioners' sugar, sifted*
• *juice of 1 large lemon, or
   2 tablespoons boiling water*
• *gel food coloring of your choice*

Put the sifted confectioners' sugar in a bowl and add the liquid slowly, a little at a time. Stir until smooth (stop adding the liquid once the icing is a smooth, spreadable consistency).

Oscar Party Cupcakes

Preparation Time 45 minutes • Cooking Time 15–20 minutes, plus cooling • Makes 12 •
Per Cupcake 336 calories, 14g fat (8g saturated), 53g carbohydrates, 300mg sodium • A Little Effort

¾ cup (1½ sticks) unsalted butter,
    at room temperature
¾ cup plus 2 tablespoons superfine
    sugar
3 large eggs
1⅓ cups plus 1 tablespoon all-
    purpose flour, sifted
1¼ teaspoons baking powder
1 teaspoon vanilla extract

FOR THE TOPPING
confectioners' sugar, for dusting
7 ounces white fondant icing
3 ounces black fondant icing
3 ounces yellow fondant icing
tools—round cutter

1. Preheat the oven to 350°F. Line a 12-cup muffin pan with paper muffin liners. Using a hand mixer, beat the butter and superfine sugar in a bowl, or beat with a wooden spoon, until pale and creamy. Gradually beat in the eggs until just combined.

2. Fold in the flour, baking powder, and vanilla, and stir well to combine. Divide the batter evenly among the paper liners and bake for 15–20 minutes until risen and springy to the touch. Transfer to a wire rack to cool completely.

3. On a counter lightly dusted with confectioners' sugar, roll out the white fondant icing to a thickness of ⅛ inch. Cut out 12 circles using a 3-inch cutter. Brush each circle with water and place on the top of each cake.

4. On a counter lightly dusted with confectioners' sugar, roll out the black fondant icing to a thickness of ⅛ inch. Cut out six bow ties and jacket shapes, and place on each cake to make the black suits. Place 3 small round circles on the jackets to make the buttons.

5. Using the yellow fondant, shape six Oscars. Place a small strip of black fondant icing on the bottom of each Oscar and attach each one to the top of each cupcake.

St. Patrick's Day Cupcakes

Preparation Time 30 minutes • Cooking Time 15–20 minutes, plus cooling • Makes 12 •
Per Cupcake 300 calories, 14g fat (8g saturated), 43g carbohydrates, 300mg sodium • A Little Effort

¾ cup (1½ sticks) unsalted butter,
    at room temperature
¾ cup plus 2 tablespoons superfine
    sugar
3 large eggs
1⅓ cups plus 1 tablespoon all-
    purpose flour, sifted
1¼ teaspoons baking powder
1 tablespoon vanilla extract

FOR THE TOPPING
confectioners' sugar, for dusting
7 ounces white fondant icing
1 ounce bright green fondant icing
tools—round cutter

1. Preheat the oven to 350°F. Line a 12-cup muffin pan with paper muffin liners. Using a hand mixer, beat the butter and superfine sugar in a bowl, or beat with a wooden spoon, until pale and creamy. Gradually beat in the eggs until just combined.

2. Fold in the flour, baking powder, and vanilla, and stir well to combine. Divide the batter evenly among the paper liners and bake for 15–20 minutes until pale golden, risen, and springy to the touch. Transfer to a wire rack to cool completely.

3. On a counter lightly dusted with confectioners' sugar, roll out the white fondant icing to a thickness of ⅛ inch. Cut out 12 circles using a 2½-inch cutter. Dampen one side of each fondant circle with a few drops of water and place, dry side up, on the cakes.

4. On a counter lightly dusted with confectioners' sugar, roll out the bright green fondant icing to a thickness of ⅛ inch. Cut out 12 shamrock shapes from the icing. Brush the white fondant icing with a little water and arrange a shamrock on each disk.

Easter Sunday Cupcakes

Preparation Time 30 minutes • Cooking Time 30 minutes, plus cooling and setting • Makes 6 •
Per Cupcake 378 calories, 27g fat (8g saturated), 32g carbohydrates, 200mg sodium • Easy

2 large eggs

¼ cup plus 2 tablespoons superfine sugar

⅔ cup sunflower oil

1⅛ cups plus 4 teaspoons all-purpose flour, sifted

½ teaspoon baking powder

1 teaspoon vanilla extract

½ cup puffed rice cereal

FOR THE TOPPING

3½ ounces white chocolate, broken into pieces

1 tablespoon unsalted butter

½ cup puffed rice cereal

12 chocolate mini eggs

1. Preheat the oven to 350°F. Line a 6-cup muffin pan with paper muffin liners.

2. Separate the eggs, putting the whites in a clean, grease-free bowl and the yolks in another. Add the sugar to the yolks and beat with a hand mixer until pale and creamy. Then beat in the oil until combined.

3. Whisk the egg whites until soft peaks form. Using a metal spoon, quickly fold the flour, baking powder, vanilla extract, and puffed rice cereal into the egg yolk mixture until just combined. Add half the egg whites to the egg yolk mixture to loosen, and then carefully fold in the remaining egg whites. Divide the batter equally between the paper liners.

4. Bake for 20–25 minutes until golden and risen. Leave to cool in the pan for 5 minutes, and then transfer to a wire rack to cool completely.

5. For the topping, put the chocolate and butter into a heatproof bowl and place over a pot of barely simmering water, making sure the bottom of the bowl doesn't touch the water. Gently heat until the chocolate has melted, stirring occasionally until smooth. Remove the bowl from the heat, add the puffed rice cereal and fold through until coated. Spoon the mixture on top of each cake, pressing down lightly. Then top each with two chocolate eggs. Stand the cakes upright on the wire rack and leave for about 1 hour to set.

TO STORE
Store in an airtight container. They will keep for 3–5 days.

FREEZING TIP
To freeze Complete the recipe to the end of step 4. Open-freeze, and then wrap and freeze.
To use Thaw for about 1 hour, and then complete the recipe.

Mother's Day Cupcakes

Preparation Time 20 minutes • Cooking Time 10–12 minutes, plus cooling and setting • Makes 20 minis •
Per Cupcake 107 calories, 5g fat (3g saturated), 16g carbohydrates, 50mg sodium • Easy

7 tablespoons unsalted butter, softened
½ cup superfine sugar
¾ cup plus 1 tablespoon all-purpose flour
¾ teaspoon baking powder
2 large eggs

FOR THE TOPPING
generous 1 cup confectioners' sugar, sifted
pink and green food coloring
sprinkles

1. Preheat the oven to 400°F. Put 20 mini paper muffin or cupcake liners into the holes of a mini muffin or cupcake pan. If you don't have one, put the liners (two liners thick) directly on a baking sheet.

2. Put the butter, sugar, flour, baking powder, and eggs into a large bowl and beat with a wooden spoon until mixed. Divide the batter equally between the paper liners.

3. Bake for 10–12 minutes or until golden and a skewer inserted into the center comes out clean. Transfer the cakes (still in their liners) to a wire rack to cool completely.

4. Divide the sifted confectioners' sugar between two bowls. If using liquid food coloring, add a little pink to one bowl and green to the other, and then stir to check the consistency. To each bowl, add just enough water to bring the mixture together to a smooth, spoonable consistency. If using coloring pastes, dye white icings, already at the right consistency, by dipping the end of a toothpick into dyes, and then into the icing. Stir to mix.

5. Cover top of each cake with green or pink icing. Top with sprinkles. Serve or leave to set first.

Memorial Day Cupcakes

Preparation Time 35 minutes • Cooking Time 15–20 minutes, plus cooling • Makes 12 •
Per Cupcake 379 calories, 14g fat (8g saturated), 64g carbohydrates, 400mg sodium • A Little Effort

¾ cup (1½ sticks) unsalted butter,
    at room temperature
¾ cup plus 2 tablespoons superfine
    sugar
1⅓ cups plus 1 tablespoon all-
    purpose flour, sifted
1¼ teaspoons baking powder
1 teaspoon vanilla extract

FOR THE TOPPING
confectioners' sugar, for dusting
7 ounces white fondant icing
7 ounces blue fondant icing
3½ ounces red fondant icing
tools—round cutter and small star
    cutter

1. Preheat the oven to 350°F. Line a 12-cup muffin pan with paper muffin liners. Using a hand mixer, beat the butter and superfine sugar in a bowl, or beat with a wooden spoon, until pale and creamy. Gradually beat in the eggs until just combined.

2. Fold in the flour, baking powder, and vanilla, and stir well to combine. Divide the batter evenly among the paper liners and bake for 15–20 minutes until pale golden, risen, and springy to the touch. Transfer to a wire rack to cool completely.

3. On a counter lightly dusted with confectioners' sugar, roll out the white and blue fondant icing to a thickness of ⅛ inch. Cut out six circles with a 3-inch round cutter with each color.

4. Place a circle on top of each cupcake. Roll out the red fondant to a thickness of ⅛ inch and, using a knife, cut out ½-inch strips. Place 3 strips on top of each white fondant circle.

5. Using the remainder of the white fondant icing, cut out small stars using the star cutter. Place 10–12 stars on top of the cupcakes with the blue fondant.

Independence Day Cupcakes

Preparation Time 30 minutes • Cooking Time 20 minutes, plus cooling and setting • Makes 12 •
Per Cupcake 254 calories, 10g fat (2g saturated), 42g carbohydrates, 400mg sodium • Easy

1 cup all-purpose flour

2 teaspoons baking powder

½ cup plus 2 tablespoons superfine
    sugar

½ cup (1 stick) soft margarine or
    butter

2 extra-large eggs

grated zest of 2 large unwaxed
    lemons (see Cook's Tip on
    page 162)

1 tablespoon freshly squeezed
    lemon juice

FOR THE TOPPING

2 cups confectioners' sugar, sifted

juice of 1 large lemon, or
    2 tablespoons boiling water

2 tablespoons royal icing (see
    right)

gel food colorings

edible glitter (optional)

multicolored dragées

1. Preheat the oven to 375°F.
Line a 12-cup muffin pan with
paper muffin liners.

2. Sift the flour, baking powder,
and sugar into a large bowl, food
processor, or mixer. Add the butter
or margarine, eggs, lemon zest, and
juice, and beat until light and fluffy.

3. Spoon the batter into the liners
and bake for about 20 minutes
until firm to the touch and golden.
Transfer to a wire rack to cool
completely.

4. For the topping, put the sifted
confectioners' sugar in a bowl and
add the liquid slowly, a little at a
time. Stir until smooth (stop adding
the liquid once the icing is a smooth,
spreadable consistency).

5. Separate the royal icing into as
many bowls as you want colors, and
tint them accordingly with the food
coloring. Using pastry bags with
fine tips, pipe on whatever fireworks
you like, such as wheels, rockets,
and shooting stars.

6. Sprinkle a tiny bit of edible glitter
over them if you want, and add the
dragées, which may need a tiny dab
of royal icing underneath them to
hold them in place.

COOK'S TIP

Royal Icing

- *1 extra-large egg white*
- *1¼ cups confectioners' sugar,
  sifted*
- *1 teaspoon freshly squeezed
  lemon juice*

*Put all the ingredients into a bowl,
and stir until the mixture is smooth
and stands in stiff peaks. If the
mixture is too stiff, add a few drops
of lemon juice or boiling water. If it
is too runny, add a little more sifted
confectioners' sugar. The icing can
be made in advance and stored in
the fridge for up to 3 days. Cover
with plastic wrap and store in an
airtight container.*

Yankee Doodle Cupcakes

Preparation Time 30 minutes • Cooking Time 15–20 minutes, plus cooling • Makes 12 •
Per Cupcake 462 calories, 24g fat (15g saturated), 62g carbohydrates, 300mg sodium • A Little Effort

¾ cup (1½ sticks) unsalted butter,
  at room temperature
¾ cup plus 2 tablespoons superfine
  sugar
3 large eggs
1⅓ cups plus 1 tablespoon all-
  purpose flour, sifted
1¼ teaspoons baking powder
1 teaspoon vanilla extract

FOR THE TOPPING
½ cup (1 stick) unsalted butter,
  at room temperature
2½ cups confectioners' sugar,
  sifted
2–3 tablespoons warm water
2 ounces white fondant icing
2 ounces blue fondant icing
2 ounces red fondant icing
12 mini American flags
tools—mini star cutter

1. Preheat the oven to 350°F. Line
a 12-cup muffin pan with paper
muffin liners. Using a hand mixer,
beat the butter and superfine sugar
in a bowl, or beat with a wooden
spoon, until pale and creamy.
Gradually beat in the eggs until
just combined.

2. Fold in the flour, baking powder,
and vanilla, and stir well to
combine. Divide the batter evenly
among the paper liners and bake
for 15–20 minutes until pale golden,
risen, and springy to the touch.
Transfer to a wire rack to cool
completely.

3. For the topping, place the butter
in a bowl and cream until soft.
Gradually beat the confectioners'
sugar plus the warm water into the
butter until smooth.

4. Transfer the frosting to a pastry
bag fitted with a large star tip and
pipe a swirl of frosting over each
cake. Using the three different
colors of fondant icing, cut out small
stars and sprinkle a few of each
color over the frosting. Top with
an American flag.

Halloween Cupcakes

Preparation Time 30 minutes, plus drying • Cooking Time 20 minutes, plus cooling • Makes 12 •
Per Cupcake 257 calories, 10g fat (2g saturated), 42g carbohydrates, 400mg sodium • A Little Effort

1 cup all-purpose flour

2 teaspoons baking powder

½ cup plus 2 tablespoons superfine sugar

½ cup (1 stick) soft margarine or butter

2 extra-large eggs

grated zest of 2 large unwaxed lemons (see Cook's Tip on page 162)

1 tablespoon freshly squeezed lemon juice

FOR THE TOPPING

candied icing (see Cook's Tip page 87)

black and orange food coloring paste

3½ ounces black fondant icing

3½ ounces white fondant icing

edible glue

small paintbrush

1. Preheat the oven to 375°F. Line a 12-cup muffin pan with paper muffin liners.

2. Sift the flour, baking powder, and sugar into a large bowl, food processor, or mixer. Add the butter or margarine, eggs, lemon zest, and juice and beat until light and fluffy.

3. Spoon the batter into the liners and bake for about 20 minutes until firm to the touch and golden. Transfer to a wire rack to cool

4. For the topping, make the candied icing and divide into two portions; use the food coloring to make one black and the other deep orange. Divide the cupcakes into two batches, and ice one batch black and the other batch orange. Leave them to dry completely.

5. Divide the white fondant icing into six parts and make a ghost from each piece by flattening out into the shape of a ghost. Use edible glue to stick it onto a black-iced cupcake. Let the ghost trail over the edge of the cake. Take some tiny bits of black fondant icing, and stick them on to make a creepy face for the ghost.

6. Make the spider using a bit of black fondant icing the size of a fava bean, and stick it onto an orange-iced cake using edible glue. Make eight legs out of slivers of black paste, and stick them on the top. Create a face and fangs out of white fondant icing. For the eyes, take two elongated egg shapes of white fondant icing, add black pupils, and stick onto an orange-iced cake.

Trick or Treat Cupcakes

Preparation Time 30 minutes • Cooking Time 15–20 minutes, plus cooling • Makes 12 •
Per Cupcake 586 calories, 20g fat (12g saturated), 105g carbohydrates, 500mg sodium • A Little Effort

¾ cup (1½ sticks) unsalted butter, at room temperature

¾ cup plus 2 tablespoons superfine sugar

3 large eggs

1⅓ cups plus 1 tablespoon all-purpose flour, sifted

1¼ teaspoons baking powder

4 tablespoons canned pumpkin puree

2 teaspoons ground cinnamon

½ teaspoon ground ginger

FOR THE TOPPING

⅔ cup cream cheese

2 tablespoons pumpkin puree

2 teaspoons ground cinnamon

7 cups confectioners' sugar, sifted, plus extra for dusting

3½ ounces orange fondant icing

black icing pen

mini silver sugar stars, to decorate (optional)

1. Preheat the oven to 350°F. Line a 12-cup muffin pan with paper muffin liners. Using a hand mixer, beat the butter and superfine sugar in a bowl, or beat with a wooden spoon, until pale and creamy. Gradually beat in the eggs until just combined.

2. Fold in the flour, baking powder, pumpkin puree, cinnamon, and ginger, and stir well to combine. Divide the batter evenly among the paper liners and bake for 15–20 minutes until risen and springy to the touch. Transfer to a wire rack to cool completely.

3. To make the topping, place the cream cheese in a bowl and soften with a fork. Stir in the pumpkin puree and cinnamon. Gradually beat in the confectioners' sugar, until smooth. Transfer the frosting to a pastry bag fitted with a fat plain tip and pipe a mound onto each cake.

4. On a counter lightly dusted with confectioners' sugar, roll out the orange fondant icing to a thickness of ⅛ inch. Cut out 12 pumpkin shapes and draw in the details with a black icing pen. Place each pumpkin on top of the frosting. Decorate each cake with mini sugar stars (optional).

Day of the Dead Cupcakes

Preparation Time 30 minutes • Cooking Time 15–20 minutes, plus cooling • Makes 12 •
Per Cupcake 336 calories, 14g fat (8g saturated), 53g carbohydrates, 300mg sodium • A Little Effort

¾ cup (1½ sticks) unsalted butter,
    at room temperature
¾ cup plus 2 tablespoons superfine
    sugar
3 large eggs
1⅓ cups plus 1 tablespoon all-
    purpose flour, sifted
1¼ teaspoons baking powder
1 teaspoon vanilla extract

FOR THE TOPPING
confectioners' sugar, for dusting
7 ounces black fondant icing
5 ounces white fondant icing
icing pens in various colors

1. Preheat the oven to 350°F. Line a 12-cup muffin pan with paper muffin liners. Using a hand mixer, beat the butter and superfine sugar in a bowl, or beat with a wooden spoon, until pale and creamy. Gradually beat in the eggs until just combined.

2. Fold in the flour, baking powder, and vanilla and stir well to combine. Divide the batter evenly among the paper liners and bake for 15–20 minutes until risen and springy to the touch. Transfer to a wire rack to cool completely.

3. On a counter lightly dusted with confectioners' sugar, roll out the black fondant icing to a thickness of ⅛ inch. Cut out 12 circles using a 3-inch plain cutter. Brush each circle with water and place on the top of each cake.

4. On a counter lightly dusted with confectioners' sugar, roll out the white fondant icing to a thickness of ⅛ inch. Cut out 12 skull shapes. Brush each shape with water and place on the top of each black circle.

5. Draw the skull features in place using the icing pens.

Christmas Cupcakes

Preparation Time 20 minutes • Cooking Time 20 minutes, plus cooling and setting • Makes 12 •
Per Cupcake 268 calories, 10g fat (6g saturated), 45g carbohydrates, 400mg sodium • Easy

¼ cup plus 2 teaspoons raisins

2 tablespoons rum or brandy*

4 ounces candied cherries

½ cup (1 stick) unsalted butter,
  softened

½ cup plus 2 tablespoons superfine
  sugar

2 extra-large eggs

1 cup all-purpose flour

2 teaspoons baking powder

½ teaspoon apple pie spice

FOR THE TOPPING

white fondant icing

2 tablespoons royal icing (see
  Cook's Tip page 100)

silver dragées

1. Put the raisins and brandy or rum into a small bowl and set aside for 1 hour. Preheat the oven to 350°F. Line a 12-cup muffin pan with paper muffin liners. Rinse the candied cherries, pat dry, and then roughly chop.

2. Put the butter and sugar in a bowl and beat together until light and fluffy. Beat the eggs in a separate bowl with a hand mixer, and gradually add to the butter and sugar mixture, beating well between each addition. Add the contents of the bowl containing the soaked raisins, and beat well.

3. Sift the flour, baking powder, and mixed spice onto a large plate, and toss the chopped cherries into the flour. Carefully add to the wet mixture, and fold in with a large metal spoon. Spoon carefully into the paper liners and bake for 20 minutes until golden and firm to the touch. Transfer to a wire rack to cool completely.

4. For the topping, make the fondant icing and use to ice the cupcakes. Leave to set.

5. Put the royal icing into a pastry bag, and pipe Christmas tree shapes onto the cakes. Add silver dragées to the trees as decorations.

* This recipe is not suitable for children because it contains alcohol.

Sweet 16 Cupcakes

Preparation Time 15 minutes • Cooking Time 20 minutes, plus cooling and setting • Makes 12 •
Per Cupcake 233 calories, 10g fat (2g saturated), 36g carbohydrates, 400mg sodium • Easy

1 cup all-purpose flour, sifted
½ cup plus 2 tablespoons superfine sugar, sifted
½ cup (1 stick) soft margarine or butter
2 teaspoons baking powder
2 extra-large eggs
1 teaspoon vanilla extract

FOR THE TOPPING
1¾ cups confectioners' sugar, sifted
gel food coloring
12 sugar roses

1. Preheat the oven to 350°F. Line a 12-cup muffin pan with paper muffin liners.

2. Put the flour, sugar, baking powder, margarine or butter, eggs, and vanilla in a mixer and beat until the mixture is pale and creamy.

3. Divide the batter into the paper liners and bake for 20 minutes or until golden, and firm and springy to the touch. Transfer the cakes to a wire rack to cool completely.

4. For the topping, put the confectioners' sugar in a bowl and slowly add enough boiling water until you have a thick soup consistency. Add the food coloring and pour over the cupcakes. Leave for about 10 minutes before carefully placing a rose on top of each cupcake.

COOK'S TIP
Sugar roses are made from flower paste and can be bought from confectionery shops. They are also readily available from online confectionery shops in a variety of colors and sizes.

Quinceañera Cupcakes

Preparation Time 35 minutes • Cooking Time 20 minutes, plus cooling • Makes 12 • Per Cupcake 361 calories, 14g fat (6g saturated), 58g carbohydrates, 200mg sodium • Easy

5 ounces raw beets, peeled and finely grated

1½ cups plus 2 tablespoons all-purpose flour, sifted

1½ teaspoons baking powder

½ teaspoon baking soda

¾ cup superfine sugar

zest of 1 unwaxed orange (see Cook's Tip on page 162)

2 large eggs

⅓ cup plus 1 tablespoon sunflower oil

½ cup buttermilk

FOR THE TOPPING

7 tablespoons unsalted butter, softened

3 cups confectioners' sugar, sifted

¼ cup milk

pink food coloring

ready-made pink or red sugar flowers (optional)

1. Preheat the oven to 375°F. Line a 12-cup muffin pan with paper muffin liners.

2. Put the beets, flour, baking powder, baking soda, superfine sugar, and orange zest into a bowl. Put the eggs, oil, and buttermilk into another bowl and lightly beat together until combined. Pour the egg mixture into the flour and stir with a spatula until just combined. Divide the batter equally between the paper liners.

3. Bake for 20 minutes or until lightly golden and risen. Leave to cool in the pan for 5 minutes, and then transfer to a wire rack to cool completely.

4. For the topping, put the butter into a bowl and beat until fluffy. Gradually beat in half the confectioners' sugar, and then add the milk, a little pink food coloring, and the remaining confectioners' sugar and beat until light and fluffy.

5. Insert a star tip into a pastry bag, and then fill the bag with the buttercream and pipe small swirls all the way around the top of each cake. Decorate with the sugar flowers, if using.

TO STORE
Store in an airtight container. They will keep for 3–5 days.

FREEZING TIP
To freeze Complete the recipe to the end of step 3. Open-freeze, and then wrap and freeze.
To use Thaw for about 1 hour, and then complete the recipe.

Wedding Cupcakes

Preparation Time 30 minutes • Cooking Time 15 minutes, plus cooling and setting • Makes 12 •
Per cupcake 375 calories, 20g fat (12g saturated), 50g carbohydrates, 600mg sodium • Easy

1 cup all-purpose flour, sifted
2 teaspoons baking powder
½ cup plus 2 tablespoons superfine
  sugar
½ cup (1 stick) unsalted butter,
  softened
2 large eggs
1 tablespoon milk

FOR THE TOPPING
⅔ cup (1⅓ sticks) unsalted butter,
  at room temperature
2¾ cups confectioners' sugar,
  sifted
2 tablespoons milk
pink food coloring paste
12 rose-themed cupcake surrounds

1. Preheat the oven to 400°F. Put paper liners into 18 of the cups in two muffin pans.

2. Put the flour, baking powder, sugar, butter, eggs, and milk into a mixing bowl and mix with a hand mixer for 2 minutes or until the batter is pale and very soft. Fill each paper liner halfway with the batter.

3. Bake for 10–15 minutes until golden brown. Transfer to a wire rack to cool completely.

4. To make the buttercream, put the butter, confectioners' sugar, and milk into a large bowl and beat with the hand mixer. Dip the tip of a toothpick into the desired shade of pink food coloring, and then dip into the buttercream. Use a spatula to start mixing in the color, stopping when the buttercream is marbled.

5. Fit a pastry bag with a ½-inch open-star tip and fill with the buttercream. Hold the pastry bag just above the center of a cupcake and start piping with even pressure. Swirl the frosting in a spiral from the center towards the edges, making sure the entire surface of the cake is covered. By starting in the center (rather than the outside edge as is normal) you should create a rose effect. Repeat with the remaining cupcakes. Leave to set for at least 1 hour.

6. Fit the surrounds around the cupcakes.

COOK'S TIPS

It is best to decorate these cupcakes on the day that they're needed, but the undecorated cakes can be made and frozen ahead. Bake, cool, and freeze the cupcakes up to one month before the event. When needed, allow the cakes to thaw at room temperature before decorating.

For added wow-factor, roll out colored fondant icing (ideally mixed with gum tragacanth, a natural gum you can get from specialist cake shops or via websites) until ¼ inch thick, and then stamp out small heart shapes. You could even pipe the initials of the bride and groom onto the hearts. Stick the hearts (standing upright) into the top edge of each frosted cupcake.

Pearl Anniversary Cupcakes

Preparation Time 35 minutes • Cooking Time 15–20 minutes, plus cooling • Makes 12 •
Per Cupcake 419 calories, 25g fat (15g saturated), 51g carbohydrates, 300mg sodium • Easy

¾ cup (1½ sticks) unsalted butter,
   at room temperature
¾ cup plus 2 tablespoons superfine
   sugar
3 large eggs
1⅓ cups plus 1 tablespoon all-
   purpose flour, sifted
1¼ teaspoons baking powder
1 teaspoon vanilla extract

FOR THE TOPPING
½ cup (1 stick) unsalted butter, at
   room temperature
2–3 tablespoons warm water
2½ cups confectioners' sugar,
   sifted
ivory pearl dragées
edible glitter
12 mixed mini edible violas

1. Preheat the oven to 350°F. Line a 12-cup muffin pan with paper muffin liners. Using a hand mixer, beat the butter and superfine sugar in a bowl, or beat with a wooden spoon, until pale and creamy. Gradually beat in the eggs until just combined.

2. Fold in the flour, baking powder, and vanilla, and stir well to combine. Divide the batter evenly among the paper liners and bake for 15–20 minutes until pale golden, risen, and springy to the touch. Transfer to a wire rack to cool completely.

3. To make the topping, place the butter in a bowl and cream until soft. Gradually beat the confectioners' sugar plus the warm water into the butter until smooth.

4. Divide the buttercream between the twelve cakes and swirl over the top of each cake using a small frosting spatula. Decorate each cupcake with a sprinkling of ivory pearl dragées and edible glitter, and top with an edible viola.

Ruby Anniversary Cupcakes

Preparation Time 30 minutes • Cooking Time 15–20 minutes, plus cooling • Makes 12 •
Per Cupcake 419 calories, 24g fat (15g saturated), 51g carbohydrates, 300mg sodium • Easy

¾ cup (1½ sticks) unsalted butter,
    at room temperature
¾ cup plus 2 tablespoons superfine
    sugar
3 large eggs
1⅓ cups plus 1 tablespoon all-
    purpose flour, sifted
1¼ teaspoons baking powder
1 teaspoon vanilla extract

FOR THE TOPPING
½ cup (1 stick) unsalted butter,
    at room temperature
2½ cups confectioners' sugar,
    sifted
2–3 tablespoons warm water
dried strawberry pieces
red heart shaped sprinkles

1. Preheat the oven to 350°F. Line a 12-cup muffin pan with paper muffin liners. Using a hand mixer, beat the butter and superfine sugar in a bowl, or beat with a wooden spoon, until pale and creamy. Gradually beat in the eggs until just combined.

2. Fold in the flour, baking powder, and vanilla, and stir well to combine. Divide the batter evenly among the paper liners and bake for 15–20 minutes until pale golden, risen, and springy to the touch. Transfer to a wire rack to cool completely.

3. For the topping, place the butter in a bowl and cream until soft. Gradually beat the confectioners' sugar plus the warm water into the butter until smooth.

4. Fit a pastry bag with a ½-inch open-star tip and fill with the buttercream. Hold the pastry bag just above the center of a cupcake and start piping with even pressure. Swirl the frosting in a spiral from the center towards the edges. Repeat with the remaining cupcakes. Leave to set for at least 2 hours. Sprinkle the dried strawberry pieces and the heart sprinkles all over the cakes.

Golden Anniversary Cupcakes

Preparation Time 45 minutes • Cooking Time 15–20 minutes, plus cooling • Makes 12 • Per Cupcake 342 calories, 18g fat (10g saturated), 45g carbohydrates, 300mg sodium • A Little Effort

¾ cup (1½ sticks) unsalted butter, at room temperature

¾ cup plus 2 tablespoons superfine sugar

3 large eggs

1⅛ cups plus 4 teaspoons all-purpose flour, sifted

1 teaspoon baking powder

¼ cup plus 1 teaspoon ground almonds

finely grated zest of 1 unwaxed lemon (see Cook's Tip on page 162)

juice of ½ lemon

FOR THE TOPPING

3½ ounces good quality white chocolate bar

confectioners' sugar, for dusting

7 ounces white fondant icing

edible gold leaf

mini golden edible stars

tools—round cutter and piece of chocolate transfer sheet

1. Preheat the oven to 350°F. Line a 12-cup muffin pan with paper muffin liners. Using a hand mixer, beat the butter and superfine sugar in a bowl, or beat with a wooden spoon, until pale and creamy. Gradually beat in the eggs until just combined.

2. Fold in the flour, baking powder, and almonds. Add the lemon zest and juice ,and stir well to combine. Divide the batter evenly among the paper liners and bake for 15–20 minutes until pale golden, risen, and springy to the touch. Transfer to a wire rack to cool completely.

3. Make a small pastry bag using a triangle of parchment paper. Slowly melt three-quarters of the white chocolate in a small bowl set over a pan of gently simmering water. Make sure the bottom of the bowl doesn't touch the water. Check the temperature of the chocolate with a kitchen thermometer. When it reaches 113°F, remove the bowl from the pan and stir to make sure all the chocolate has melted. Add the remaining chocolate to the bowl while stirring constantly until the chocolate cools down to 82–84°F.

4. Pour the tempered chocolate into the pastry bag, cut off the tip, and pipe the number '50' onto a chocolate transfer sheet. Let completely set before carefully peeling off. Keep refrigerated until use.

5. On a counter lightly dusted with confectioners' sugar, roll out the white fondant icing to a thickness of ⅛ inch. Cut out 12 round disks using a 2-inch cutter. Dampen one side of each fondant circle with a few drops of water and place, dry side up, on the cakes.

6. Make two small indentations in the fondant and brush a very small amount of water inside. Carefully press the tempered chocolate 50s into the indentations so they stand upright. Add small pieces of edible gold leaf over the top of each disk using a sharp knife, and add gold sugar stars.

KIDS'
CUPCAKES

Vanilla Cupcakes

Preparation Time 15 minutes • Cooking Time 20 minutes, plus cooling and setting • Makes 12 •
Per Cupcake 255 calories, 15g fat (9g saturated), 29g carbohydrates, 110mg sodium • Easy

½ cup (1 stick) unsalted butter,
   softened

½ cup plus 2 tablespoons superfine
   sugar

2 large eggs

1 cup all-purpose flour

1 teaspoon baking powder

1 teaspoon vanilla extract

FOR THE TOPPING

7 ounces white chocolate, broken
   into pieces

1. Preheat the oven to 375°F. Line a 12-cup muffin pan with paper muffin liners.

2. Put the butter, sugar, eggs, flour, baking powder, and vanilla into a large bowl and beat thoroughly until smooth and creamy. Fill the paper liners halfway with the batter and bake for 15–20 minutes or until pale golden, risen, and springy to the touch. Transfer to a wire rack to cool completely.

3. For the topping, melt the chocolate in a heatproof bowl set over a pan of gently simmering water, making sure the bottom of the bowl doesn't touch the water. Stir until smooth, and then leave to cool slightly. Spoon the chocolate over the cakes and leave for about 1 hour to set.

Jeweled Cupcakes

Preparation Time 40 minutes • Cooking Time 30 minutes, plus cooling and setting • Makes 12 •
Per Cupcake 276 calories, 10g fat (4g saturated), 46g carbohydrates, 400mg sodium • Easy

**6 tablespoons unsalted butter,
  softened**
¾ cup superfine sugar
3 large eggs
**1⅓ cups plus 1 tablespoon all-
  purpose flour, sifted**
1¼ teaspoons baking powder
6 ounces mincemeat

FOR THE TOPPING
**¼ cup apricot glaze (see Cook's
  Tip on page 33)**
½ cup toasted flaked almonds
¼ cup dried apricots, chopped
12 candied cherries
¼ cup superfine sugar
1 tablespoon cold water
1 tablespoon unsalted butter

1. Preheat the oven to 375°F. Line
a 12-cup muffin pan with paper
muffin liners.

2. Using a hand mixer, beat the
butter and sugar in a bowl, or beat
with a wooden spoon, until pale and
creamy. Gradually beat in the eggs
until just combined. Using a metal
spoon, fold in the flour, baking
powder, and mincemeat until
combined. Divide the batter
equally between the paper liners.

3. Bake for 20 minutes or until
golden and risen. Leave to cool in
the pan for 5 minutes, and then
transfer to a wire rack to cool
completely.

4. For the topping, brush each
cake with a little apricot glaze and
scatter on a few almonds, apricots,
and a cherry. Stand the cakes
upright on a wire rack.

5. Put the sugar and the cold water
into a small pan and gently heat
until the sugar dissolves. Increase
the heat and bubble for 3–4 minutes
until the sugar caramelizes and
turns golden in color. Remove from
the heat and quickly stir in the
butter until combined. Carefully
drizzle the hot caramel over the
top of each cake. Leave for about
10 minutes to set.

TO STORE
*Store in an airtight container. They
will keep for 3–5 days.*

FREEZING TIP
To freeze *Complete the recipe to
the end of step 3. Open-freeze, and
then wrap and freeze.*
To use *Thaw for about 1 hour, and
then complete the recipe.*

Superhero Cupcakes

Preparation Time 35 minutes • Cooking Time 15–20 minutes, plus cooling • Makes 12 •
Per Cupcake 407 calories, 14g fat (8g saturated), 72g carbohydrates, 300mg sodium • A Little Effort

¾ cup (1½ sticks) unsalted butter,
    at room temperature
¾ cup plus 2 tablespoons superfine
    sugar
3 large eggs
1⅓ cups plus 1 tablespoon all-
    purpose flour, sifted
1¼ teaspoons baking powder
1 teaspoon vanilla extract

FOR THE TOPPING
confectioners' sugar, for dusting
7 ounces blue fondant icing
3 ounces yellow fondant icing
5 ounces green fondant icing
5 ounces orange fondant icing
5 ounces purple fondant icing
5 ounces black fondant icing

1. Preheat the oven to 350°F. Line a 12-cup muffin pan with paper muffin liners. Using a hand mixer, beat the butter and superfine sugar in a bowl, or beat with a wooden spoon, until pale and creamy. Gradually beat in the eggs until just combined.

2. Fold in the flour, baking powder, and vanilla, and stir well to combine. Divide the batter evenly among the paper liners and bake for 15–20 minutes until risen and springy to the touch. Transfer to a wire rack to cool completely.

3. On a counter lightly dusted with confectioners' sugar, roll out the blue and yellow fondant icing to a thickness of ⅛ inch. Cut out 6 circles of each color using a 3-inch cutter. Brush each circle with water and place on the top of each cake.

4. On a counter lightly dusted with confectioners' sugar, roll out the green, orange, and purple fondant icing to a thickness of ⅛ inch. With a small knife, cut out a starburst shape. Brush each one with water and place on top of each cake.

5. On a counter lightly dusted with confectioners' sugar, roll out the black fondant icing to a thickness of ⅛ inch. Cut out words such as "pow," "zap," and "bam" to place on top of the starbursts. Brush each one with water and place on top of the starbursts.

Woodland Forest Cupcakes

Preparation Time 50 minutes • Cooking Time 15–20 minutes, plus cooling • Makes 12 •
Per Cupcake 528 calories, 24g fat (15g saturated), 79g carbohydrates, 300mg sodium • A Little Effort

¾ cup (1½ sticks) unsalted butter,
   at room temperature
¾ cup plus 2 tablespoons superfine
   sugar
3 large eggs
1⅓ cups plus 1 tablespoon all-
   purpose flour, sifted
1¼ teaspoons baking powder
1 teaspoon vanilla extract

FOR THE TOPPING
½ cup (1 stick) unsalted butter,
   at room temperature
2½ cups confectioners' sugar,
   sifted
2–3 tablespoons warm water
3–4 drops green food coloring
4 ounces white fondant icing
6 ounces red fondant icing
1½ ounces pink fondant icing
1½ ounces yellow fondant icing

1. Preheat the oven to 350°F. Line a 12-cup muffin pan with paper muffin liners. Using a hand mixer, beat the butter and superfine sugar in a bowl, or beat with a wooden spoon, until pale and creamy. Gradually beat in the eggs until just combined.

2. Fold in the flour, baking powder, and vanilla, and stir well to combine. Divide the batter evenly among the paper liners and bake for 15–20 minutes until risen and springy to the touch. Transfer to a wire rack to cool completely.

3. For the topping, place the butter in a bowl and cream until soft. Gradually beat the confectioners' sugar plus the green coloring and the warm water into the butter until smooth.

4. Transfer the frosting to a pastry bag fitted with a medium ribbon tip and pipe green strips of grass over each cupcake.

5. To make the toadstools, divide the white and red fondant icing into 12 equal pieces. Roll each piece of white fondant icing into a stalk shape. Place a tiny blob of water on the top of each stalk. Roll each piece of red fondant icing into a ball and flatten to make the top of the toadstool. Place each top carefully in place. Roll the white fondant icing into tiny balls and flatten. Brush the red top of each toadstool with water and stick the white circles in place. Make small flowers out of the pink and yellow fondant icing.

6. Place the toadstools and flowers around each cupcake on top of the green grass frosting.

All Aboard Cupcakes

Preparation Time 45 minutes • Cooking Time 15–20 minutes, plus cooling • Makes 12 •
Per Cupcake 579 calories, 14g fat (8g saturated), 117g carbohydrates, 400mg sodium • A Little Effort

¾ cup (1½ sticks) unsalted butter,
   at room temperature
¾ cup plus 2 tablespoons superfine
   sugar
3 large eggs
1⅓ cups plus 1 tablespoon all-
   purpose flour, sifted
1¼ teaspoons baking powder
1 teaspoon vanilla extract

FOR THE TOPPING
confectioners' sugar, for dusting
7 ounces white fondant icing
7 ounces black fondant icing
7 ounces blue fondant icing
7 ounces yellow fondant icing
7 ounces red fondant icing
silver sugar balls

1. Preheat the oven to 350°F. Line a 12-cup muffin pan with paper muffin liners. Using a hand mixer, beat the butter and superfine sugar in a bowl, or beat with a wooden spoon, until pale and creamy. Gradually beat in the eggs until just combined.

2. Fold in the flour, baking powder, and vanilla, and stir well to combine. Divide the batter evenly among the paper liners and bake for 15–20 minutes until pale golden, risen, and springy to the touch. Transfer to a wire rack to cool completely.

3. On a counter lightly dusted with confectioners' sugar, roll out the white fondant icing to a thickness of ⅛ inch. Cut out 12 circles with a 3-inch round cutter. Place a white circle on the top of each cupcake.

4. Roll out the black fondant to a thickness of ⅛ inch. Cut out strips to ½ inch thick and place two long strips along the sides of each cupcake. Connect the two strips with 5–6 strips of black fondant to form the train tracks.

5. Dust your hands with confectioners' sugar and shape 3½ ounces of the blue, yellow, or red fondant into a block 5 x ½ x ½ inch. Cut the block into 12 equal pieces to form the front of the trains. Shape the remaining fondant of the same color of your choice into a block 2½ x ½ x ½ inch. Cut this block into 6 equal pieces and then cut each block in half, to give 12 pieces. Shape small round logs (about 1 ounce each) for the train chimneys. Roll 24 white dots and place them under the chimney and on the grill. Roll four black dots of fondant and place on the sides of the train to make the wheels. Place a silver ball in the middle of each black wheel. Cut a small rectangular base for the trains from the remaining fondant. Place the train on top of the base.

6. Using a bit of water attach a train to each train track cupcake.

Outer Space Cupcakes

Preparation Time 45 minutes • Cooking Time 15–20 minutes, plus cooling • Makes 12 •
Per Cupcake 336 calories, 14g fat (8g saturated), 53g carbohydrates, 300mg sodium • A Little Effort

¾ cup (1½ sticks) unsalted butter,
   at room temperature
¾ cup plus 2 tablespoons
   superfine sugar
3 large eggs
1⅓ cups plus 1 tablespoon
   all-purpose flour, sifted
1¼ teaspoons baking powder
2 ounces mini M&M's

FOR THE TOPPING
confectioners' sugar, for dusting
7 ounces gray fondant icing
3½ ounces red fondant icing
3½ ounces yellow fondant icing
3½ ounces blue fondant icing
3½ ounces green fondant icing
2 ounces white fondant icing

1. Preheat the oven to 350°F. Line a 12-cup muffin pan with 12 paper muffin liners. Using a hand mixer, beat the butter and superfine sugar in a bowl, or beat with a wooden spoon, until pale and creamy. Gradually beat in the eggs until just combined.

2. Fold in the flour, baking powder, and M&M's, and stir well to combine. Divide the batter evenly among the paper liners and bake for 15–20 minutes until pale golden, risen, and springy to the touch. Transfer to a wire rack to cool completely.

3. On a counter lightly dusted with confectioners' sugar, roll out the gray fondant icing to a thickness of ⅛ inch. Cut out 12 3-inch circles with a round cutter. Brush one side of each shape with water and place, damp side down, on the cakes.

4. On a counter lightly dusted with confectioners' sugar, roll out the red fondant icing to a thickness of ⅛ inch. Cut out 6 rocket shapes, 3 inches long. Brush one side of each shape with water and place, damp side down, on the cakes. Roll out the yellow, blue, and green fondant in the same way. Cut out moons, planets, and martians, and place on each cupcake. Cut out small stars from the white fondant icing and place 3–5 on each cupcake around the fondant cutouts.

Teddy Bear Cupcakes

Preparation Time 45 minutes • Cooking Time 15–20 minutes, plus cooling • Makes 12 •
Per Cupcake 385 calories, 14g fat (8g saturated), 66g carbohydrates, 300mg sodium • A Little Effort

¾ cup (1½ sticks) unsalted butter,
   at room temperature
¾ cup plus 2 tablespoons superfine
   sugar
3 large eggs
1⅓ cups plus 1 tablespoon all-
   purpose flour, sifted
1¼ teaspoons baking powder
1 teaspoon unsweetened cocoa
   powder

FOR THE TOPPING
confectioners' sugar, for dusting
9 ounces brown fondant icing
2 ounces pink fondant icing
3½ ounces light brown fondant
   icing
1 ounce black fondant icing
3½ ounces white fondant icing
black icing pen

1. Preheat the oven to 350°F. Line a 12-cup muffin pan with 12 paper muffin liners. Using a hand mixer, beat the butter and superfine sugar in a bowl, or beat with a wooden spoon, until pale and creamy. Gradually beat in the eggs until just combined.

2. Fold in the flour, baking powder, and cocoa powder, and stir well to combine. Divide the batter evenly among the paper liners and bake for 15–20 minutes until risen and springy to the touch. Transfer to a wire rack to cool completely.

3. On a counter lightly dusted with confectioners' sugar, roll out the brown fondant icing to a thickness of ⅛ inch. From the brown icing cut out 12 x 2½-inch circles for the face of the bear and 12 x ¾-inch circles for the ears. Cut the ¾-inch circles in half. Cut smaller circles, about ½ inch, out of the pink fondant. Cut the pink circles in half and place on top of the small brown ear circles.

4. From the light brown fondant icing, cut out 12 x ¾-inch circles to make the nose of the bears. From the brown fondant icing break off 12 small balls to finish the nose of the bears. Make 24 small balls with the black fondant to make the eyes, pressing them flat.

5. To assemble the teddy faces, brush each brown circle with a little water and position in the center of each cake. Stick the brown half circles on, with a little more water, for ears. Brush water on one side of the pink inner ears and place the damp side over the ears.

6. Brush the teddy faces and ears with water and position the eyes and the light brown noses. Carefully draw the mouth on with the black icing pen.

Dinosaur Cupcakes

Preparation Time 45 minutes • Cooking Time 15–20 minutes, plus cooling • Makes 12 •
Per Cupcake 566 calories, 24g fat (15g saturated), 89g carbohydrates, 300mg sodium • A Little Effort

¾ cup (1½ sticks) unsalted butter,
    at room temperature

¾ cup plus 2 tablespoons superfine
    sugar

3 large eggs

1⅓ cups plus 1 tablespoon all-
    purpose flour, sifted

1¼ teaspoons baking powder

1 teaspoon vanilla extract

**FOR THE FILLING AND
TOPPING**

10 tablespoons unsalted butter

2⅓ cups plus 1 tablespoon
    confectioners' sugar, sifted,
    plus extra for dusting

2–3 tablespoons warm water

5 drops green food color

14 ounces blue fondant icing

2 ounces black fondant icing

14 ounces purple fondant icing

3 ounces white fondant icing

14 ounces yellow fondant icing

14 ounces green fondant icing

14 ounces orange fondant icing

14 ounces red fondant icing

1. Preheat the oven to 350°F. Line a 12-cup muffin pan with 12 paper muffin liners. Using a hand mixer, beat the butter and superfine sugar in a bowl, or beat with a wooden spoon, until pale and creamy. Gradually beat in the eggs until just combined.

2. Fold in the flour, baking powder, and vanilla, and stir well to combine. Divide the batter evenly among the paper liners and bake for 15–20 minutes until pale golden, risen, and springy to the touch. Transfer to a wire rack to cool completely.

3. For the topping, place the butter in a bowl and cream until soft. Gradually beat the confectioners' sugar plus the warm water into the butter until smooth. Mix in the green food coloring.

4. Transfer the frosting to a pastry bag fitted with a small round tip and pipe green strips of grass over each cupcake.

5. Begin making your dinosaur figures. Using different color fondants, make a variety of different shaped dinosaurs of your choice. Using a toothpick, poke out the nose on the dinosaurs and shape the mouths. Roll out small circles for the eyes. When you finish your dinosaur fondant figures place one on top of the green grass of each cupcake.

T-REX

1. For the T-Rex, roll a small oval shape for the head and a larger oval shape for the body using blue fondant icing.

2. With the larger oval, pull one end down into a pointed tail. Attach the small oval to the body of the T-Rex using a brush of water.

3. Using a small knife, make a small slit where you would like the mouth of the T-Rex to form. Pry open a space to add the teeth.

4. Take a small piece of white fondant to fit inside the T-Rex's mouth. Squish the ball into the space formed with the knife. Brush the inside of the mouth with water and push the ball in to fit. Using the small knife, imprint a crisscross pattern to form the teeth.

5. Use 2 small balls of black fondant for the eyes. Roll 2 sausage shapes for the arms and the same sausage shapes, but half the size for the legs.

DINOSAUR

1. Take a piece of purple fondant and roll it into a log shape to form the worm dinosaur. Cut the log into 2 pieces. Take 1 piece and turn one end into a point and the other flat so it can stand on its own.

2. Take the second piece and round off one end for the face. Using a knife, make a slit where the mouth will form. Pry it open with the knife. Take 2 small balls of white fondant to form the eyes with 2 small dots of black fondant on top.

3. Make 2 indents in the top of the cupcake to hold each end of your worm. Place the 2 worm pieces in the holes and pipe icing grass around to make it look like he is peeking out of the grass.

TOROSAURUS

1. For the torosaurus, roll a small oval shape for the head and a larger oval shape for the body using yellow fondant.

2. With the larger oval, pull one end down into a pointed tail. Attach the small oval to the body of the torosaurus using a brush of water.

3. Using a small knife make a small slit where you would like the mouth to form. Using a toothpick, make 2 holes for the nose. Using 2 small balls of white fondant, make the eyes and place 2 smaller balls of black fondant on top.

4. Roll out 2 small sausage shapes for the arms and attach with a brush of water.

5. Using green fondant, cut out a spiked crown to wrap around the neck of the torosaurus and attach with a brush of water.

6. Place the torosaurus on the cupcake and pipe the grass around him.

STEGOSAURUS

1. Roll 1 large piece of orange fondant into a sausage shape to form the body of the stegosaurus rounding off one end to make the tail. Attach a small round piece of orange fondant with a brush of water. Form the eyes with 2 small balls of white fondant with 2 small dots of black fondant on top.

2. Take 4 small pieces of orange fondant and roll them into sausage shapes to form the arms and legs of the stegosaurus. Attach these with a brush of water.

3. To form the red spikes, roll out some red fondant icing to ⅛ inch thick. Cut out spikes and a flat edge on the bottom. On the flat edge, brush water to attach the spikes to the back of the stegosaurus.

4. Place the stegosaurus on top of the cupcake and pipe green icing around him so he is lying on the grass.

Secret Garden Cupcakes

Preparation Time 45 minutes • Cooking Time 40 minutes, plus cooling • Makes 12 • Per Cupcake 398 calories, 20g fat (13g saturated), 53g carbohydrates, 500mg sodium • Easy

1⅓ cups fresh strawberries, hulled and halved

1 cup superfine sugar

10 tablespoons unsalted butter, softened

3 large eggs

1½ cups plus 2 tablespoons all-purpose flour, sifted

1½ teaspoons baking powder

½ teaspoon baking soda

⅛ cup plus 1 tablespoon buttermilk

FOR THE TOPPING

½ cup (1 stick) unsalted butter, softened

2¼ cups confectioners' sugar, sifted

green food coloring

ladybug, bumblebee, and butterfly sugar decorations (optional)

1. Preheat the oven to 375°F. Line a 12-cup muffin pan with paper muffin liners.

2. Put the strawberries and ¼ cup superfine sugar into a double boiler. Cover with a lid, put over a pot of barely simmering water, and cook gently for 30 minutes.

3. Meanwhile, using a hand mixer, beat the butter and remaining superfine sugar in a bowl, or beat with a wooden spoon, until pale and creamy. Gradually beat in the eggs until just combined. Using a metal spoon, fold in the flour, baking powder, baking soda, and buttermilk until combined. Divide the batter equally between the paper liners.

4. Bake for 20 minutes or until golden and risen. Leave to cool in the pan for 5 minutes. Meanwhile, pass the strawberries and juice through a strainer into a shallow bowl. Discard the strawberries.

5. Using a toothpick, prick the top of the cakes all over. Dip the top of each cake into the strawberry syrup, and then transfer to a wire rack to cool completely.

6. For the topping, put the butter into a bowl and beat until fluffy. Gradually beat in half the confectioners' sugar. Then add 1 tablespoon boiling water, a little green food coloring, and the remaining confectioners' sugar and beat until light and fluffy.

7. Insert a star tip into a pastry bag. Then fill the bag with the buttercream and pipe in a zigzag pattern on top of each cake. Decorate with the sugar ladybugs, butterflies, and bumblebees, if you like.

TO STORE

Store in an airtight container. They will keep for 2–3 days.

Circus Cupcakes

Preparation Time 35 minutes • Cooking Time 15–20 minutes, plus cooling • Makes 12 •
Per Cupcake 379 calories, 14g fat (8g saturated), 64g carbohydrates, 300mg sodium • A Little Effort

¾ cup (1½ sticks) unsalted butter,
    at room temperature
¾ cup plus 2 tablespoons superfine
    sugar
3 large eggs
1⅓ cups plus 1 tablespoon all-
    purpose flour, sifted
1¼ teaspoons baking powder
1 teaspoon vanilla extract

FOR THE TOPPING
confectioners' sugar, for dusting
7 ounces white fondant icing
7 ounces red fondant icing
3½ ounces yellow fondant icing
12 mini flags

1. Preheat the oven to 350°F. Line a 12-cup muffin pan with paper muffin liners. Using a hand mixer, beat the butter and superfine sugar in a bowl, or beat with a wooden spoon, until pale and creamy. Gradually beat in the eggs until just combined.

2. Fold in the flour, baking powder, and vanilla, and stir well to combine. Divide the batter evenly among the paper liners and bake for 15–20 minutes until pale golden, risen, and springy to the touch. Transfer to a wire rack to cool completely.

3. On a counter lightly dusted with confectioners' sugar, roll out the white fondant icing to a thickness of ⅛ inch. Stamp out 12 x 3-inch circles and repeat with the red fondant icing.

4. Cut the red circles into 8 equal size slices. Place 5 slices on top of the white circles to make the circus tents, about ¼ inch apart. Make 12 small balls out of the yellow fondant icing and press them into the center where all of the red triangle tips meet.

5. Top each cake with a mini flag on the center of each cake.

Moustache Cupcakes

Preparation Time 30 minutes • Cooking Time 15–20 minutes, plus cooling • Makes 12 •
Per Cupcake 349 calories, 15g fat (9g saturated), 55g carbohydrates, 300mg sodium • A Little Effort

¾ cup (1½ sticks) unsalted butter,
   at room temperature
¾ cup plus 2 tablespoons superfine
   sugar
3 large eggs
1⅓ cups plus 1 tablespoon all-
   purpose flour, sifted
1¼ teaspoons baking powder
1 teaspoon vanilla extract

FOR THE TOPPING

1¾ cups confectioners' sugar,
   sifted, plus extra for dusting
4–6 teaspoons warm water
3½ ounces black fondant icing
2 ounces mini M&M's

SPECIAL EQUIPMENT

small cardboard moustache
   templates (printed from the
   internet)

1. Preheat the oven to 350°F. Line a 12-cup muffin pan with 12 paper muffin liners. Using a hand mixer, beat the butter and superfine sugar in a bowl, or beat with a wooden spoon, until pale and creamy. Gradually beat in the eggs until just combined.

2. Fold in the flour, baking powder, and vanilla extract, and stir well to combine. Divide the batter evenly among the paper liners and bake for 15–20 minutes until pale golden, risen, and springy to the touch. Transfer to a wire rack to cool completely.

3. Put the confectioners' sugar in a bowl and gradually add the warm water, 1 teaspoon at a time, beating well until the frosting is smooth and will coat the back of a spoon. Cover each cake with a layer of frosting.

4. On a counter lightly dusted with confectioners' sugar, roll out the fondant icing to a thickness of ⅛ inch. Using the moustache templates, cut out 12 moustache shapes. Place a frosting moustache on the center of each cake with a brush of water on the back, and arrange mini M&M's around the edge of each cake.

Chocolate Sundae Cupcakes

Preparation Time 35 minutes • Cooking Time 15–20 minutes, plus cooling • Makes 12 •
Per Cupcake 605 calories, 32g fat (20g saturated), 80g carbohydrates, 400mg sodium • Easy

¾ cup (1½ sticks) unsalted butter,
　at room temperature
¾ cup plus 2 tablespoons
　superfine sugar
3 large eggs
1⅓ cups plus 1 tablespoon
　all-purpose flour, sifted
1¼ teaspoons baking powder
¼ cup unsweetened cocoa powder,
　sifted

FOR THE TOPPING

1 cup (2 sticks) unsalted butter,
　at room temperature
4 cups confectioners' sugar, sifted
2–3 tablespoons warm water
2 ounces chocolate sauce
2 ounces multicolored sprinkles
¼ cup mini marshmallows
4 chocolate flakes, each cut into
　3 pieces

1. Preheat the oven to 350°F. Line a 12-cup muffin pan with paper muffin liners. Using a hand mixer, beat the butter and superfine sugar in a bowl, or beat with a wooden spoon, until pale and creamy. Gradually beat in the eggs until just combined.

2. Fold in the flour, baking powder, and cocoa powder, and stir well to combine. Divide the batter evenly among the paper liners and bake for 15–20 minutes until risen and springy to the touch. Transfer to a wire rack to cool completely.

3. For the topping, place the butter in a bowl and cream until soft. Gradually beat the confectioners' sugar plus the warm water into the butter until smooth.

4. Transfer the frosting to a pastry bag fitted with a large round tip and pipe large swirls of frosting on the cakes to look like ice cream.

5. Place a small dollop of chocolate sauce on top of each cupcake. Scatter the sprinkles on top of the chocolate sauce as well as a few mini marshmallows. Top each cupcake with a chocolate flake.

Sticky Gingerbread Cupcakes

Preparation Time 35 minutes • Cooking Time 20 minutes, plus cooling • Makes 9 • Per Cupcake 386 calories, 17g fat (11g saturated), 58g carbohydrates, 500mg sodium • Easy

1⅓ cups plus 1 tablespoon all-purpose flour

1¼ teaspoons baking powder

6 tablespoons unsalted butter, chilled and cut into cubes

¼ teaspoon baking soda

2 teaspoons ground ginger

1 ounce preserved ginger in syrup, finely chopped, plus

   3 tablespoons syrup from the jar

¼ cup packed dark brown sugar

⅛ cup plus 1 teaspoon light corn syrup

⅛ cup plus 1 teaspoon molasses

juice of 1 orange

2 large eggs, beaten

FOR THE TOPPING

7 tablespoons unsalted butter, softened

1¾ cups confectioners' sugar, sifted

3 tablespoons syrup from the preserved ginger jar

1 teaspoon ground ginger

ready-made sugar flowers (optional)

1. Preheat the oven to 375°F. Line a 12-cup muffin pan with nine paper muffin liners.

2. Put the flour and baking powder into a large bowl and, using your fingertips, rub in the butter until it resembles bread crumbs. Stir in the baking soda, ground ginger, and preserved ginger, and set aside. Put the brown sugar, syrup, molasses, and orange juice into a small saucepan and heat gently until the sugar dissolves. Leave to cool for 5 minutes.

3. Mix the eggs and warm sugar mixture into the flour mixture and stir with a spatula until just combined. Divide the batter equally between the paper liners.

4. Bake for 20 minutes or until golden and risen. Remove from the oven and drizzle each cake with 1 teaspoon ginger syrup. Leave to cool in the pan for 5 minutes, and then transfer to a wire rack to cool completely.

5. For the topping, put the butter into a bowl and beat until fluffy. Add the confectioners' sugar, ginger syrup, and ground ginger. Beat until light and fluffy. Using a small spatula, spread a little buttercream over the top of each cake. Decorate with sugar flowers, if desired.

TO STORE
Store in an airtight container. They will keep for 3–5 days.

FREEZING TIP
To freeze Complete the recipe to the end of step 4. Open-freeze, and then wrap and freeze.
To use Thaw for about 1 hour, and then complete the recipe.

Fairy Cakes

Preparation Time 20 minutes • Cooking Time 10–15 minutes, plus cooling and setting • Makes 18 •
Per Cupcake 160 calories, 6g fat (4g saturated), 26g carbohydrates, 200mg sodium • Easy

1 cup all-purpose flour, sifted
2 teaspoons baking powder
½ cup plus 2 tablespoons superfine
   sugar
½ cup (1 stick) unsalted butter,
   softened
2 large eggs
1 tablespoon milk

FOR THE TOPPING
2 cups confectioners' sugar, sifted
2–3 tablespoons warm water
assorted food colorings (optional)
candies, sprinkles, or colored
   sugar

1. Preheat the oven to 400°F. Line two 12-cup muffin pans with 18 paper muffin liners.

2. Put the flour, baking powder, sugar, butter, eggs, and milk into a mixing bowl and mix with a hand mixer for 2 minutes or until the batter is pale and very soft. Fill each paper liner halfway with the batter.

3. Bake for 10–15 minutes until golden brown. Transfer to a wire rack to cool completely.

4. For the topping, put the confectioners' sugar into a bowl and gradually blend in the warm water until the icing is fairly stiff, but spreadable. Add a couple of drops of food coloring, if desired.

5. When the cakes are cooled, spread the tops with the icing and decorate.

TO STORE
Store in an airtight container. They will keep for 3–5 days.

FREEZING TIP
To freeze *Complete the recipe to the end of step 3. Open-freeze, and then wrap and freeze.*
To use *Thaw for about 1 hour, and then complete the recipe.*

Chocolate Butterfly Cakes

Preparation Time 25 minutes • Cooking Time 15–20 minutes, plus cooling • Makes 18 • Per Cupcake 170 calories, 7g fat (4g saturated), 26g carbohydrates, 200mg sodium • Easy

½ cup (1 stick) unsalted butter, softened

½ cup plus 2 tablespoons superfine sugar

2 large eggs, lightly beaten individually

1 cup all-purpose flour

¼ cup unsweetened cocoa powder

½ teaspoon baking powder

1 tablespoon milk

1 x quantity of buttercream (see page 159)

1. Preheat the oven to 375°F. Line two 12-cup muffin pans with 18 paper muffin liners.

2. Using a hand mixer, beat the butter and sugar together until soft and fluffy and lighter in color. Beat in the eggs thoroughly, one at a time.

3. Sift the flour, cocoa powder, and baking powder into the bowl and fold in gently until well mixed. Fold in the milk to give a soft, dropping consistency. Divide the batter equally between the paper liners.

4. Bake for 15–20 minutes until risen and firm. Transfer to a wire rack to cool completely.

5. Slice off the top of each cake and cut the slice in half. Using a spatula, spread buttercream on each cake. Put the "butterfly wings" on top, with their curved sides facing towards each other.

TO STORE
Store in an airtight container. They will keep for up to 2 days.

COOK'S TIP
Color the buttercream with pink or green food coloring if you like, to match the theme of the party.

Chocolate Fairy Cakes

Preparation Time 20 minutes • Cooking Time 10–15 minutes, plus cooling and setting • Makes 18 •
Per Cupcake 171 calories, 7g fat (4g saturated), 28g carbohydrates, 300mg sodium • Easy

¾ cup plus 1 tablespoon all-
  purpose flour
¼ cup unsweetened cocoa powder
1¾ teaspoons baking powder
½ cup plus 2 tablespoons superfine
  sugar
½ cup (1 stick) unsalted butter,
  softened
2 large eggs
1 tablespoon milk
¼ cup chocolate chips

FOR THE TOPPING
2 cups confectioners' sugar, sifted
2–3 tablespoons warm water
assorted food colorings (optional)
candies, sprinkles, or colored
  sugar

1. Preheat the oven to 400°F.
Line two 12-cup muffin pans with
18 paper muffin liners.

2. Sift the flour into a mixing bowl.
Then sift in the cocoa powder,
baking powder, and sugar. Add
the butter, eggs, and milk and beat
with a hand mixer for 2 minutes or
until the mixture is pale and very
soft. Stir in the chocolate chips,
and spoon into the paper liners.

3. Bake for 10–15 minutes until
risen and springy to the touch.
Transfer to a wire rack to cool
completely.

4. For the frosting, put the
confectioners' sugar into a bowl
and gradually blend in the warm
water until the frosting is fairly stiff,
but spreadable. Add a couple of
drops of food coloring, if desired.

5. Spread the tops of the cakes
with the frosting and decorate with
candies, sprinkles, or colored
sugar.

Kitten Cupcakes

Preparation Time 25 minutes • Cooking Time 20 minutes, plus cooling • Makes 12 • Per Cupcake 223 calories, 10g fat (6g saturated), 34g carbohydrates, 200mg sodium • Easy

½ cup (1 stick) unsalted butter, softened
½ cup plus 2 tablespoons superfine sugar
grated zest of 1 unwaxed lemon (see Cook's Tip on page 162)
2 large eggs, beaten
1 cup all-purpose flour, sifted
1 teaspoon baking powder

FOR THE TOPPING
1½ cups confectioners' sugar
2–3 tablespoons warm water
assorted writing icings
gumdrops and sugar-coated chocolate candies
black licorice laces, cut into short lengths

1. Preheat the oven to 375°F. Line a 12-cup muffin pan with paper muffin liners.

2. Put the butter, superfine sugar, and lemon zest into a mixing bowl and, using a hand mixer, beat until pale and fluffy. Add the eggs, a little at a time, beating well after each addition. Fold in the flour and baking powder. Divide the batter between the paper liners. Bake for about 20 minutes or until golden and risen. Transfer to a wire rack to cool completely.

3. Sift the confectioners' sugar into a bowl. Stir in the warm water, a few drops at a time, until you have a smooth, spreadable icing. If necessary, slice the tops off the cooled cupcakes to make them level. Cover the top of each cake with icing.

4. Decorate the cakes to make kittens' faces. Use black writing icing for the eyes, halve the gumdrops for the ears, press a candy in the center for a nose, and use black writing icing to draw on a mouth. Use different colored writing icing for the pupils and markings. Press on licorice whiskers.

TO STORE
Store in an airtight container. They will keep for 3–5 days.

FREEZING TIP
To freeze *Complete the recipe to the end of step 2. Open-freeze, and then wrap and freeze.*
To use *Thaw for about 1 hour, and then complete the recipe.*

Red Nose Cupcakes

Preparation Time 20 minutes • Cooking Time 12–15 minutes, plus cooling and setting • Makes 36 minis •
Per Cupcake 39 calories, 1g fat (1g saturated), 7g carbohydrates, trace sodium • Easy

**4 tablespoons unsalted butter,
  softened**
¼ cup superfine sugar
1 large egg, beaten
**⅓ cup plus 1 tablespoon all-
  purpose flour**
½ teaspoon baking powder
1 ripe banana, peeled and mashed

FOR THE TOPPING
1 cup confectioners' sugar, sifted
1 tablespoon orange juice
**red candied cherries or round red
  jelly candies**

1. Preheat the oven to 375°F.
Arrange about 36 mini paper muffin
liners on baking sheets.

2. Put the butter, superfine sugar,
egg, flour, and baking powder into
a food processor and process until
smooth and well mixed. Add the
banana and process for 1 minute.
Put a teaspoonful of the batter into
each paper liner.

3. Bake for 12–15 minutes until
golden. Transfer to a wire rack
to cool completely.

4. For the icing, mix the
confectioners' sugar with the
orange juice until smooth and just
thick enough to coat the back of
a spoon. Top each cupcake with a
small blob of icing and stick half
a cherry or a candy on each one.
Stand the cakes upright on a wire
rack and leave for about 1 hour
to set.

TO STORE
*Store in an airtight container. They
will keep for 3–5 days.*

FREEZING TIP
To freeze *Complete the recipe to
the end of step 3. Open-freeze, and
then wrap and freeze.*
To use *Thaw for about 1 hour, and
then complete the recipe.*

Polka Dot Cupcakes

Preparation Time 30 minutes • Cooking Time 20 minutes, plus cooling • Makes 12 • Per Cupcake 283 calories, 12g fat (4g saturated), 42g carbohydrates, 200mg sodium • Easy

2 cups all-purpose flour, sifted
1 tablespoon baking powder
½ cup superfine sugar
1 teaspoon vanilla extract
2 large eggs
½ cup sunflower oil
¾ cup plain yogurt

FOR THE TOPPING
4 tablespoons unsalted butter, softened
1½ cups confectioners' sugar, sifted
¼ cup unsweetened cocoa powder, sifted
2 tablespoons boiling water
mini sugar-coated chocolates or chocolate chips

1. Preheat the oven to 375°F. Line a 12-cup muffin pan with paper muffin liners.

2. Put the flour, baking powder, and superfine sugar into a large bowl. Put the vanilla extract, eggs, oil, and yogurt into a bowl and lightly beat together until combined. Pour into the flour mixture and stir with a spatula until just combined. Divide the batter equally between the paper liners.

3. Bake for 20 minutes or until lightly golden and risen. Leave to cool in the pan for 5 minutes, and then transfer to a wire rack to cool completely.

4. For the topping, put the butter into a bowl and beat until fluffy. Gradually add the confectioners' sugar until combined. Add the unsweetened cocoa powder and the boiling water, and beat until light and fluffy. Using a small spatula, spread a little buttercream over the top of each cake. Decorate with mini sugar-coated chocolate candies or chocolate chips.

TO STORE
Store in an airtight container. They will keep for 3–5 days.

FREEZING TIP
To freeze *Complete the recipe to the end of step 3. Open-freeze, and then wrap and freeze.*
To use *Thaw for about 1 hour, and then complete the recipe.*

Easy Peasy Chocolate Cupcakes

Preparation Time 25 minutes • Cooking Time 15 minutes • Makes 12 • Per Cupcake 410 calories, 23g fat (14g saturated), 51g carbohydrates, 100mg sodium • Easy

⅔ cup (1⅓ sticks) unsalted butter, softened

¾ cup superfine sugar

3 large eggs, at room temperature

1 teaspoon vanilla extract

1½ cups all-purpose flour

1½ teaspoons baking powder

¼ cup unsweetened cocoa powder

pinch of salt

FOR THE BUTTERCREAM

⅔ cup (1⅓ sticks) unsalted butter, at room temperature

2¾ cups confectioners' sugar, sifted

2 tablespoons milk

1. Preheat oven to 375°F. Line a 12-cup muffin pan with paper muffin liners. To make the cakes, put the butter and superfine sugar into a large bowl. Crack in the eggs and add the vanilla extract. Sift over flour, baking powder, cocoa powder, and a pinch of salt.

2. Beat the ingredients together using an hand mixer. Then divide mixture among the liners. Bake for 15–20 minutes until firm and a toothpick inserted into the center comes out clean. Cool on a wire rack.

3. To make the buttercream, put the butter, confectioners' sugar, and milk into a large bowl and beat with the hand mixer. Spread over the cooled cupcakes and serve.

Dark Chocolate Cupcakes

Preparation Time 15 minutes • Cooking Time 20 minutes, plus cooling and setting • Makes 18 •
Per Cupcake 203 calories, 14g fat (8g saturated), 19g carbohydrates, 200mg sodium • Easy

½ **cup (1 stick) unsalted butter,**
   softened
½ **cup plus 2 tablespoons packed**
   light brown sugar
2 **large eggs, beaten**
⅛ **cup plus 1 teaspoon**
   unsweetened cocoa powder
¾ **cup plus 1 tablespoon all-**
   purpose flour
¾ **teaspoon baking powder**
3½ **ounces dark chocolate, roughly**
   chopped

FOR THE TOPPING
⅔ **cup heavy cream**
3½ **ounces dark chocolate**
   (at least 70% cocoa solids),
   broken up

1. Preheat the oven to 375°F. Line two 12-cup muffin pans with 18 paper muffin liners.

2. Beat the butter and sugar together until light and fluffy. Gradually beat in the eggs. Sift the unsweetened cocoa powder with the flour and baking powder and fold into the creamed mixture with the chopped chocolate. Divide the batter among the paper liners and lightly flatten the surface with the back of a spoon.

3. Bake for 20 minutes, and then transfer to a wire rack to cool completely.

4. For the topping, put the cream and chocolate into a heavy pan over low heat and heat until melted. Then allow to cool and thicken slightly. Spoon onto the cooled cakes, and then stand the cakes upright on the wire rack and leave for 30 minutes to set.

TO STORE
Store in an airtight container in the fridge. They will keep for 2–3 days.

FREEZING TIP
To freeze Complete the recipe to the end of step 3. Open-freeze, and then wrap and freeze.
To use Thaw for about 1 hour, and then complete the recipe.

Banana Toffee Cupcakes

Preparation Time 30 minutes • Cooking Time 20 minutes, plus cooling • Makes 12 • Per Cupcake 404 calories, 16g fat (10g saturated), 63g carbohydrates, 400mg sodium • Easy

1⅓ cups plus 1 tablespoon all-purpose flour, sifted
1¼ teaspoons baking powder
½ teaspoon baking soda
¾ cup packed light brown sugar
1 ripe banana, peeled
3 large eggs
7 tablespoons unsalted butter, melted
⅓ cup buttermilk

FOR THE TOPPING
5 ounces dulce de leche toffee sauce
6 tablespoons unsalted butter, softened
2¼ cups confectioners' sugar, sifted
mini fudge chunks (optional)

1. Preheat the oven to 375°F. Line a 12-cup muffin pan with paper muffin liners.

2. Put the flour, baking powder, baking soda, and brown sugar into a large bowl. Mash the banana with a fork in a small bowl. Put the eggs, melted butter, and buttermilk into a bowl and lightly beat together until combined. Pour into the flour mixture along with the mashed banana and stir with a spatula until just combined. Divide the batter equally between the paper liners.

3. Bake for 18–20 minutes until lightly golden and risen. Leave to cool in the pan for 5 minutes, and then transfer to a wire rack to cool completely.

4. For the topping, beat together the dulce de leche and butter in a bowl until combined. Gradually beat in the confectioners' sugar until light and fluffy. Use a spatula to spread the buttercream onto the top of each cake. Decorate with the mini fudge chunks, if using.

TO STORE
Store in an airtight container. They will keep for 2–3 days.

FREEZING TIP
To freeze Complete the recipe to the end of step 3. Open-freeze, and then wrap and freeze.
To use Thaw for about 1 hour, and then complete the recipe.

Star Cupcakes

Preparation Time 40 minutes, plus drying • Cooking Time 20 minutes, plus cooling • Makes 12 •
Per Cupcake 226 calories, 10g fat (6g saturated), 34g carbohydrates, 400mg sodium • Easy

½ cup (1 stick) unsalted butter,
    softened
½ cup plus 2 tablespoons superfine
    sugar
2 extra-large eggs
grated zest and juice of 1 large
    unwaxed lemon (see Cook's Tip)
1 cup all-purpose flour
2 teaspoons baking powder

FOR THE TOPPING
1½ cups confectioners' sugar
2–3 tablespoons warm water
confectioners' sugar to dust
4 ounces white fondant icing
edible glue
edible glitter in silver and gold

1. Preheat the oven to 350°F. Line a 12-cup muffin pan with paper muffin liners.

2. Put the butter and sugar in a large bowl and beat with a hand mixer until light and fluffy. Beat the eggs in a separate bowl. Then gradually add them to the butter and sugar mixture, beating well between each addition. Add the lemon zest and beat well.

3. Sift in the flour and baking powder, and fold in with a large metal spoon. If the batter needs loosening a bit, add a little lemon juice. The batter should gently drop off a spoon. Divide the batter equally between the paper liners and bake for 20 minutes or until firm to the touch and golden. Transfer to a wire rack to cool completely.

4. For the topping, sift the confectioners' sugar into a bowl. Stir in the warm water, a few drops at a time, until you have a smooth, spreadable icing. If necessary, slice the tops off the cooled cupcakes to make them level. Cover the top of each cake with icing and leave to dry.

5. Dust a work surface with confectioners' sugar, and roll out the fondant icing until it is about ⅛ inch thick. Cut out 12 star shapes using a star-shaped cutter.

6. Paint edible glue over each star, making sure they are completely covered, before dipping six stars in gold glitter and six in silver glitter. Dab a tiny bit of edible glue on the center of each cupcake and carefully place a star on top.

COOK'S TIP
To remove the wax from a waxed citrus fruit, place the fruit in a bowl of warm water and scrub it all over with a stiff vegetable brush. Rinse thoroughly, and then pat dry.

Peanut Butter and Chocolate Cupcakes

Preparation Time 30 minutes • Cooking Time 25 minutes, plus cooling and setting • Makes 12 •
Per Cupcake 363 calories, 17g fat (7g saturated), 49g carbohydrates, 500mg sodium • Easy

½ cup unsalted peanuts or cashew
    nuts, toasted
7 tablespoons unsalted butter,
    softened
¼ cup packed light brown sugar
¼ cup packed dark brown sugar
3 large eggs
1⅓ cups plus 1 tablespoon all-
    purpose flour, sifted
1¾ teaspoons baking powder

FOR THE TOPPING
½ cup milk
½ cup unsweetened cocoa powder
2⅔ cups confectioners' sugar
⅓ cup smooth peanut butter
chocolate sprinkles

1. Preheat the oven to 375°F. Line a 12-cup muffin pan with paper muffin liners.

2. Whiz the peanuts or cashews in a food processor until finely ground. Set aside.

3. Using a hand mixer, beat the butter with the brown sugars, or beat with a wooden spoon, until pale and creamy. Gradually beat in the eggs until just combined. Using a metal spoon, fold in the flour, baking powder, and finely ground nuts until combined. Divide the batter equally between the paper liners.

4. Bake for 20 minutes or until golden and risen. Leave to cool in the pan for 5 minutes, and then transfer to a wire rack to cool completely.

5. For the topping, warm the milk in a small saucepan. Sift the cocoa and confectioners' sugar into a bowl. Gradually stir in the warm milk until it forms a smooth icing.

6. Put a small spoonful of peanut butter on the top of each cake and then spoon the chocolate icing on to cover the peanut butter and to coat the top of the cupcake. Decorate with sprinkles. Stand the cakes upright on a wire rack and leave for about 1 hour to set.

TO STORE
Store in an airtight container. They will keep for 3–5 days.

FREEZING TIP
To freeze Complete the recipe to the end of step 4. Open-freeze, and then wrap and freeze.
To use Thaw for about 1 hour, and then complete the recipe.

FRUITY
FEASTS

Citrus Cupcakes

Preparation Time 15 minutes • Cooking Time 20 minutes, plus cooling • Makes 12 •
Per Cupcake 362 calories, 21g fat (8g saturated), 42g carbohydrates, 400mg sodium • Easy

1 cup all-purpose flour
2 teaspoons baking powder
½ cup plus 2 tablespoons superfine sugar
½ cup (1 stick) soft margarine or butter
2 extra-large eggs
grated zest of 2 large unwaxed lemons (see Cook's Tip on page 162), plus extra shreds, to decorate (optional)
1 tablespoon freshly squeezed lemon juice

FOR THE TOPPING
4 ounces lemon curd
¾ cup crème fraîche

1. Preheat the oven to 375°F. Line a 12-cup muffin pan with paper muffin liners.

2. Sift the flour, baking powder, and sugar into a large bowl, food processor, or mixer. Add the butter or margarine, eggs, lemon zest, and juice, and beat until light and fluffy.

3. Spoon the batter into the liners and bake for about 20 minutes until firm to the touch and golden. Transfer to a wire rack to cool completely.

4. For the topping, use a small, sharp knife to slice the top off each cake. Then place a generous spoonful of lemon curd on top of the cake and put the lid back on.

5. Add a dollop of crème fraîche and a few shreds of lemon zest, if desired.

Tropical Burst Cupcakes

Preparation Time 35 minutes • Cooking Time 20 minutes, plus cooling and setting • Makes 12 •
Per Cupcake 256 calories, 8g fat (1g saturated), 45g carbohydrates, 200mg sodium • Easy

1½ cups plus 2 tablespoons all-purpose flour, sifted
1½ teaspoons baking powder
½ teaspoon baking soda
½ cup superfine sugar
2 ounces dried tropical fruit, finely chopped
3 large eggs
⅓ cup plus 1 tablespoon sunflower oil
⅓ cup buttermilk
1 (8-ounce) can pineapple pieces, drained and finely chopped

FOR THE TOPPING
2 cups confectioners' sugar, sifted
zest and juice of 1 unwaxed lime (see Cook's Tip on page 162)
1 tablespoon cold water
sugar decorations (optional)

1. Preheat the oven to 375°F. Line a 12-cup muffin pan with paper muffin liners.

2. Put the flour, baking powder, baking soda, superfine sugar, and dried fruit into a large bowl. Put the eggs, oil, and buttermilk into another bowl and lightly beat together until combined. Pour the oil mixture and the pineapple pieces into the flour and stir with a spatula until just combined. Divide the batter equally between the paper liners.

3. Bake for 20 minutes or until lightly golden and risen. Leave to cool in the pan for 5 minutes, and then transfer to a wire rack to cool completely.

4. For the topping, put the confectioners' sugar, lime juice and zest, and the cold water into a bowl and beat for 5 minutes or until soft peaks form. Using a small spatula, spread a little over the top of each cake. Stand the cakes upright on the wire rack, sprinkle with sugar decorations, if desired, and leave for about 1 hour to set.

TO STORE
Store in an airtight container. They will keep for 3–5 days.

FREEZING TIP
To freeze Complete the recipe to the end of step 3. Open-freeze, and then wrap and freeze.
To use Thaw for about 1 hour, and then complete the recipe.

Tangy Orange Cupcakes

Preparation Time 40 minutes • Cooking Time 15–18 minutes, plus cooling and setting • Makes 9 •
Per Cupcake 309 calories, 1g fat (0g saturated), 76g carbohydrates, 0mg sodium • Easy

1 small orange (about 7 ounces)
1⅓ cups plus 1 tablespoon all-purpose flour, sifted
2¼ teaspoons baking powder
½ cup superfine sugar
⅓ cup plus 1 tablespoon milk
1 large egg, beaten
4 tablespoons unsalted butter, melted
zest of 1 large unwaxed lemon (see Cook's Tip on page 162)

FOR THE TOPPING
3½ cups confectioners' sugar, sifted
zest and juice of 1 small unwaxed orange
sugar star sprinkles
edible glitter (optional)

1. Preheat the oven to 375°F. Line a 12-cup muffin pan with nine paper muffin liners.

2. Grate the zest from the orange into a large bowl and set aside. Cut the top and bottom off the orange and stand it upright on a board. Using a serrated knife, cut away the pith in a downward motion. Roughly chop the orange flesh, discarding any seeds. Put the chopped orange into a food processor and process until pureed.

3. Transfer the orange puree into the bowl with the zest. Add the flour, baking powder, superfine sugar, milk, egg, melted butter, and lemon zest. Stir with a spatula until just combined. Divide the batter equally between the paper liners.

4. Bake for 15–18 minutes until golden and risen. Leave to cool in the pan for 5 minutes, and then transfer to a wire rack to cool completely.

5. For the topping, put the confectioners' sugar, orange juice, and zest into a bowl and beat for 5 minutes or until soft peaks form. Spoon a little over the top of each cake to flood the top, and then sprinkle with the stars. Stand the cakes upright on the wire rack and leave for about 1 hour to set. Dust with edible glitter, if desired, when set.

TO STORE
Store in an airtight container. They will keep for 3–5 days.

FREEZING TIP
To freeze Complete the recipe to the end of step 4. Open-freeze, and then wrap and freeze.
To use Thaw for about 1 hour, and then complete the recipe.

Ginger and Lemon Cupcakes

Preparation Time 15 minutes • Cooking Time 20 minutes, plus cooling • Makes 12 •
Per Cupcake 246 calories, 10g fat (2g saturated), 40g carbohydrates, 400mg sodium • Easy

1 cup all-purpose flour

½ cup plus 2 tablespoons superfine
   sugar

½ cup (1 stick) soft margarine or
   butter

2 teaspoons baking powder

1 teaspoon ground ginger

grated zest of 1 unwaxed lemon
   (see Cook's Tip on page 162)

2 extra-large eggs

2 ounces candied ginger, chopped,
   plus extra to decorate

FOR THE TOPPING

1¾ cups confectioners' sugar,
   sifted

juice of 1 lemon

1. Preheat the oven to 375°F. Line
a 12-cup muffin pan with paper
muffin liners.

2. Sift the flour and sugar into a
large bowl, food processor, or mixer.
Add the margarine or butter, baking
powder, ground ginger, lemon zest,
and eggs, and beat well until pale
and creamy. Gently fold in the
chopped candied ginger.

3. Divide the batter equally between
the liners and bake for 20 minutes
or until golden and firm to the touch.
Transfer to a wire rack to cool
completely.

4. For the topping, put the
confectioners' sugar into a bowl.
Then slowly add the lemon juice
and mix well. If you need a little
more liquid, add a few drops of
boiling water. Spread the icing over
the cupcakes and top with a little
chunk of the extra candied ginger.

Forest Fruit Cupcakes

Preparation Time 25 minutes • Cooking Time 18–20 minutes, plus cooling • Makes 12 •
Per Cupcake 506 calories, 27g fat (17g saturated), 66g carbohydrates, 70mg sodium • Easy

¾ cup plus 2 tablespoons superfine
  sugar
¾ cup (1½ sticks) unsalted butter,
  at room temperature
3 large eggs, lightly beaten
finely grated zest of 1 lemon (see
  Cook's Tip on page 162)
1⅓ cups plus 1 tablespoon all-
  purpose flour, sifted
1 teaspoon baking powder
¼ cup plus 1 teaspoon seedless
  dark fruit preserve such as black
  currant

FOR THE TOPPING
¾ cup (1½ sticks) unsalted butter,
  at room temperature
1 teaspoon vanilla extract
3¼ cups confectioners' sugar,
  sifted
⅓ cup fresh blackberries

1. Preheat the oven to 350°F. Line a 12-cup muffin pan with paper muffin liners.

2. Using a hand mixer, beat the superfine sugar and butter in a large bowl for 3 minutes or until light and fluffy. Gradually add the eggs, whisking continuously—if the mixture looks as if it is about to curdle, add 1 tablespoon flour. Whisk in half of the lemon zest.

3. Use a large metal spoon to fold in the flour and baking powder. Divide the batter evenly between the paper liners and bake for 18–20 minutes until golden. Transfer to a wire rack to cool completely.

4. Spoon the preserve into a pastry bag fitted with a ¼-inch plain tip. Push the piping tip into the middle of the top of each cake and squeeze a little preserve into the center.

5. For the topping, put the butter, vanilla, the remaining lemon zest, and two-thirds of the confectioners' sugar into a large bowl and slowly beat with a hand mixer. Gradually beat in the remaining confectioners' sugar until you have a soft but spreadable consistency that holds its shape. Briefly whisk in the fresh blackberries to get a marbled effect.

6. Pipe or spread the frosting onto the cakes and serve.

GET AHEAD
Prepare to the end of step 3 up to a day ahead. Leave to cool completely, and then transfer the cakes to an airtight container and store at room temperature.
To use *Complete the recipe to serve.*

Brazil Nut and Clementine Cakes

Preparation Time 30 minutes, plus cooling and freezing • Cooking Time 1¼ hours, plus cooling • Makes 8 •
Per Cake 413 calories, 26g fat (5g saturated), 41g carbohydrates, 100mg sodium • Easy

butter to grease
1 lemon
10 clementines
1 cup Brazil nuts
½ cup olive oil
3 large eggs
**1⅓ cups plus 2 teaspoons
  superfine sugar**
1 teaspoon baking powder
2 tablespoons brandy*

TO DECORATE
mint sprigs
confectioners' sugar

1. Grease eight ⅔ cup ramekins and line with baking parchment. Wash the lemon and four clementines, and put into a pan. Cover with boiling water, reduce the heat to a gentle simmer, and cook for 30 minutes or until the clementines are tender.

2. Remove the clementines with a slotted spoon and set aside. Cook the lemon for another 10 minutes or until tender. Drain, reserving ¾ cup of the liquid, and cool slightly. Halve the fruit, remove the seeds, and roughly chop.

3. Preheat the oven to 350°F. Grind the nuts in a food processor until finely chopped, and then pour out and set aside. There's no need to wash the pitcher—add the cooked fruit and blend to a puree.

4. Put the oil, eggs, and ⅔ cup of the superfine sugar into a mixing bowl and whisk until slightly thick and foamy. Stir in the ground nuts, fruit puree, and baking powder. Divide among the ramekins and put on a baking sheet. Bake for 25 minutes or until slightly risen and firm to the touch. Leave to cool in the pan.

5. Peel the remaining clementines, remove the seeds, and divide into segments. Then skin each segment. Heat the remaining sugar in a small pan with ⅔ cup of the reserved cooking liquid until the sugar dissolves. Bring to a boil and cook until a pale caramel in color. Dip the bottom of the pan into cold water to stop the caramel from cooking. Stir in the remaining liquid and the brandy. Return to the heat, stirring until the caramel has dissolved. Stir in the clementine segments.

6. Loosen the edges of the cakes, turn out onto individual plates, and remove the baking parchment. Pile the fruit segments on top and spoon the caramel over them. Decorate each with a mint sprig and a dusting of confectioners' sugar.

__ This recipe is not suitable for children because it contains alcohol.__*

GET AHEAD
Make the recipe to the end of step 5. Wrap the cakes, still in their ramekins, in plastic wrap, and pour the clementines and syrup into a freezer bag. You can freeze both for up to a month.
***To use** Thaw the cakes at room temperature for 4 hours or overnight in the fridge. Finish with step 6.*

Raspberry Ripple Cupcakes

Preparation Time 30 minutes • Cooking Time 20 minutes, plus cooling • Makes 9 • Per Cupcake 385 calories, 26g fat (16g saturated), 36g carbohydrates, 500mg sodium • Easy

⅛ **cup plus 1 teaspoon seedless raspberry preserve**

⅓ **cup plus 1 tablespoon fresh raspberries**

½ **cup (1 stick) unsalted butter, softened**

½ **cup superfine sugar**

2 **large eggs**

1 **tablespoon milk**

1⅛ **cups plus 4 teaspoons all-purpose flour, sifted**

1 **teaspoon baking powder**

FOR THE TOPPING

1¼ **cups fresh raspberries**

1¼ **cups whipping cream**

½ **cup confectioners' sugar, sifted**

1. Preheat the oven to 375°F. Line a 12-cup muffin pan with paper muffin liners.

2. Mix the raspberry preserve with the raspberries, lightly crushing the raspberries. Set aside.

3. Using a hand mixer, beat the butter and superfine sugar in a bowl, or beat with a wooden spoon, until pale and creamy. Gradually beat in the eggs and milk until just combined. Using a metal spoon, fold in the flour and baking powder until just combined. Carefully fold in the raspberry preserve mixture until just marbled, being careful not to over-mix. Divide the batter equally between the paper liners.

4. Bake for 20 minutes or until golden and risen. Leave to cool in the pan for 5 minutes, and then transfer to a wire rack to cool completely.

5. For the decoration, reserve 9 raspberries. Mash the remaining raspberries in a bowl with a fork. Pass through a strainer into a bowl to remove the seeds. Using a hand mixer, beat the cream and confectioners' sugar together until stiff peaks form. Mix the raspberry puree into the cream until combined.

6. Insert a star tip into a pastry bag. Then fill the bag with the cream and pipe a swirl onto the top of each cake. Decorate each with a raspberry.

TO STORE

Store in an airtight container in the fridge. They will keep for up to 2 days.

FREEZING TIP

To freeze *Complete the recipe to the end of step 4. Open-freeze, and then wrap and freeze.*

To use *Thaw for about 1 hour, and then complete the recipe.*

Coconut and Lime Cupcakes

Preparation Time 30 minutes • Cooking Time 18–20 minutes, plus cooling and setting • Makes 12 •
Per Cupcake 291 calories, 13g fat (6g saturated), 42g carbohydrates, 100mg sodium • Easy

2⅛ cups plus 4 teaspoons
   all-purpose flour, sifted
1 tablespoon baking powder
½ cup superfine sugar
zest of 1 unwaxed lime (see Cook's
   Tip on page 162)
½ cup desiccated coconut
2 large eggs
⅓ cup plus 1 tablespoon sunflower
   oil
1 cup plain yogurt
⅛ cup plus 1 tablespoon milk

FOR THE TOPPING
1⅓ cups confectioners' sugar,
   sifted
juice of 1 lime
1–2 teaspoons boiling water
½ cup desiccated coconut

1. Preheat the oven to 400°F. Line a 12-cup muffin pan with paper muffin liners.

2. Put the flour, baking powder, superfine sugar, lime zest, and coconut into a large bowl. Put the eggs, oil, yogurt, and milk into a bowl and lightly beat together until combined. Pour the yogurt mixture into the flour and stir with a spatula until just combined. Divide the batter equally between the paper liners.

3. Bake for 18–20 minutes until lightly golden and risen. Leave to cool in the pan for 5 minutes, and then transfer to a wire rack to cool completely.

4. For the topping, mix the confectioners' sugar with the lime juice and the boiling water to make a thick, smooth icing. Put the coconut into a shallow bowl. Dip each cake top into the icing until coated, allowing the excess to drip off, and then carefully dip into the coconut until coated. Stand the cakes upright on the wire rack and leave for about 1 hour to set.

TO STORE
Store in an airtight container. They will keep for 3–5 days.

FREEZING TIP
To freeze Complete the recipe to the end of step 3. Open-freeze, and then wrap and freeze.
To use Thaw for about 1 hour, and then complete the recipe.

Orange and Poppy Seed Cupcakes

Preparation Time 30 minutes • Cooking Time 20 minutes, plus cooling • Makes 12 • Per Cupcake 408 calories, 24g fat (14g saturated), 49g carbohydrates, 500mg sodium • Easy

¾ cup (1½ sticks) unsalted butter, softened

¾ cup plus 2 tablespoons superfine sugar

3 large eggs

1⅓ cups plus 1 tablespoon all-purpose flour, sifted

1¼ teaspoons baking powder

grated zest and juice of 1 large unwaxed orange (see Cook's Tip on page 162)

2 tablespoons poppy seeds

FOR THE TOPPING

½ cup (1 stick) unsalted butter, softened

2¼ cups confectioners' sugar, sifted

1 tablespoon orange flower water

12 orange jelly slices and orange edible glitter (optional)

1. Preheat the oven to 375°F. Line a 12-cup muffin pan with paper muffin liners.

2. Mix the butter and superfine sugar in a bowl with a hand mixer, or beat with a wooden spoon, until pale and creamy. Gradually beat in the eggs until just combined. Using a metal spoon, fold in the flour, baking powder, orange zest and juice, and poppy seeds until combined. Divide the batter equally between the paper liners. Bake for 20 minutes or until golden and risen. Leave to cool in the pan for 5 minutes, and then transfer to a wire rack to cool completely.

3. For the topping, put the butter into a bowl and beat until fluffy. Gradually add the confectioners' sugar and orange flower water and mix until light and fluffy.

4. Insert a star tip into a pastry bag. Then fill the bag with the frosting and pipe a swirl onto the top of each cake. Decorate each with an orange slice and edible glitter, if desired.

TO STORE
Store in an airtight container. They will keep for 3–5 days.

FREEZING TIP
To freeze Complete the recipe to the end of step 3. Open-freeze, and then wrap and freeze.
To use Thaw for about 1 hour, and then complete the recipe.

Carrot Cupcakes

Preparation Time 30 minutes • Cooking Time 20 minutes, plus cooling • Makes 12 • Per Cupcake 255 calories, 12g fat (4g saturated), 34g carbohydrates, 300mg sodium • Easy

5 ounces carrots

¼ cup plus 2 teaspoons raisins

1¼ cups all-purpose flour, sifted

1¼ teaspoons baking powder

½ teaspoon baking soda

¾ cup packed light brown sugar

zest of 1 unwaxed orange (see Cook's Tip on page 162)

½ teaspoon apple pie spice

3 large eggs

⅓ cup plus 1 tablespoon sunflower oil

⅓ cup buttermilk

FOR THE TOPPING

½ cup confectioners' sugar, sifted

1 cup mascarpone cheese

½ cup cream cheese

juice of ½ orange

orange and green fondant icing (optional)

1. Preheat the oven to 375°F. Line a 12-cup muffin pan with paper muffin liners.

2. Coarsely grate the carrots and put into a large bowl. Add the raisins, flour, baking powder, baking soda, brown sugar, orange zest, and apple pie spice. Put the eggs, oil, and buttermilk into a bowl and lightly beat together until combined. Pour the egg mixture into the flour and stir with a spatula until just combined.

3. Divide the batter equally between the paper liners and bake for 20 minutes or until lightly golden and risen. Leave to cool in the pan for 5 minutes, and then transfer to a wire rack to cool completely.

4. For the topping, mix the sifted confectioners' sugar with the mascarpone, cream cheese, and orange juice to a smooth frosting. Using a small spatula, spread a little of the frosting over each cake. Use the colored fondant to make small carrots, if desired, and use to decorate the cakes.

Lemon and Vanilla Cupcakes

Preparation Time 25 minutes • Cooking Time 15 minutes, plus cooling • Makes 12 • Per Cupcake 387 calories, 21g fat (13g saturated), 47g carbohydrates, 600mg sodium • Easy

1 cup superfine sugar

¾ cup (1½ sticks) unsalted butter, softened

finely grated zest and juice of 1 unwaxed lemon (see Cook's Tip on page 162)

4 large eggs, beaten

1½ cups plus 2 tablespoons all-purpose flour

1½ teaspoons baking powder

FOR THE TOPPING

6 tablespoons unsalted butter, softened

1½ cups confectioners' sugar, sifted

1–2 tablespoons milk

1 teaspoon vanilla extract

Selection of sugar sprinkles

1. Preheat the oven to 400°F. Line a 12-cup muffin pan with paper muffin liners.

2. Put the sugar, butter, and lemon zest into a large bowl. Using a hand mixer, whisk together until pale and creamy. Beat in the eggs a little at a time, folding in 1 tablespoon flour if the mixture looks as if it is about to curdle.

3. Using a metal spoon, fold in the flour, baking powder, and lemon juice. Divide the batter equally between the paper liners. Bake for 12–15 minutes until golden. Transfer to a wire rack to cool.

4. For the topping, put the butter into a large bowl and beat in two-thirds of the confectioners' sugar with a hand mixer. Gradually beat in the rest of the confectioners' sugar with the milk and vanilla until you have a soft but spreadable consistency that holds its shape.

5. When the cakes are completely cooled, top each one with frosting and swirl with a flat-bladed knife to form peaks. Decorate with sugar sprinkles.

Pineapple and Coconut Cupcakes

Preparation Time 35 minutes • Cooking Time 15–20 minutes, plus cooling • Makes 12 •
Per Cupcake 492 calories, 42g fat (28g saturated), 26g carbohydrates, 300mg sodium • A Little Effort

1 (8-ounce) can pineapple in
    natural juice
¾ cup (1½ sticks) salted butter,
    at room temperature
¾ cup plus 2 tablespoons superfine
    sugar
3 large eggs
1 cup all-purpose flour, sifted
1 teaspoon baking powder
½ cup dry unsweetened coconut

FOR THE TOPPING
3 tablespoons dry unsweetened
    coconut
2 cups heavy cream, lightly
    whipped
3 ounces dried sliced coconut
    pieces

1. Preheat the oven to 350°F. Line a 12-cup muffin pan with paper muffin liners. Drain the pineapple, reserving the juice, and finely chop the fruit.

2. Using a hand mixer, beat the butter and superfine sugar in a bowl, or beat with a wooden spoon, until pale and creamy. Gradually beat in the eggs until just combined.

3. Fold in the flour, baking powder, and coconut and stir well to combine. Stir in 4 tablespoons of the reserved pineapple juice and 3½ ounces of the finely chopped pineapple. Divide the batter evenly among the paper liners and bake for 15–20 minutes until risen and springy to the touch. Transfer to a wire rack to cool completely.

4. For the topping, heat a small nonstick skillet over high heat. Add the 3 tablespoons coconut and toast until browned, give the pan a shake occasionally to prevent it from burning.

5. Stir 4 tablespoons of the reserved juice into the whipped cream. Transfer the cream to a pastry bag fitted with a large star tip and pipe a swirl of cream over each cake. Arrange a few pieces of the dried sliced coconut in each swirl and sprinkle over some of the remaining chopped pineapple. Scatter a little toasted coconut over each cake.

Rum and Raisin Cupcakes

Preparation Time 35 minutes, plus overnight soaking • Cooking Time 15–20 minutes, plus cooling • Makes 12 •
Per Cupcake 581 calories, 29g fat (18g saturated), 77g carbohydrates, 400mg sodium • A Little Effort

1 cup raisins

4 tablespoons dark rum*

¾ cup (1½ sticks) unsalted butter,
   at room temperature

¾ cup plus 2 tablespoons packed
   raw brown sugar

3 large eggs

1⅓ cups plus 1 tablespoon all-
   purpose flour, sifted

1¼ teaspoons baking powder

1 teaspoon ground cinnamon

FOR THE TOPPING

1 cup (2 sticks) unsalted butter,
   at room temperature

4 cups confectioners' sugar, sifted

2 tablespoons dark rum

FOR THE DRIZZLE

2 tablespoons raw brown sugar

2 tablespoons boiling water

1 tablespoon dark rum

1. Place the raisins and the
4 tablespoons of rum in a small
bowl and let soak overnight.

2. Preheat the oven to 350°F. Line a
12-cup muffin pan with paper muffin
liners. Using a hand mixer, beat the
butter and sugar in a bowl, or beat
with a wooden spoon, until pale and
creamy. Gradually beat in the eggs
until just combined.

3. Fold in the flour, baking powder,
and cinnamon, and stir well to
combine. Set aside one quarter
of the soaked raisins for the
decoration. Add the remaining
raisins and soaking liquid to the
cake batter and stir thoroughly.

4. Divide the batter evenly among
the paper liners and bake for
15–20 minutes until risen and
springy to the touch. Transfer to
a wire rack to cool completely.

5. For the topping, place the butter
in a bowl and cream until soft.
Gradually beat the confectioners'
sugar and rum into the butter until
smooth.

6. To make the rum drizzle,
dissolve 2 tablespoons of sugar in
2 tablespoons boiling water in a
pan, and boil down to a syrupy
consistency. Add the 1 tablespoon
rum and let cool.

7. Add 3 tablespoons of frosting
onto each cake and using a small
palette knife, work the frosting
around into a cone shape. Top each
cake with a few of the reserved
raisins and the rum drizzle.

** This recipe is not suitable for
children because it contains
alcohol.*

Strawberry Shortcake Cupcakes

Preparation Time 45 minutes • Cooking Time 25–30 minutes, plus cooling • Makes 12 •
Per Cupcake 546 calories, 44g fat (27g saturated), 35g carbohydrates, 400mg sodium • A Little Effort

FOR THE SHORTBREAD

¼ cup (½ stick) salted butter

2 tablespoons superfine sugar

½ cup all-purpose flour, plus extra
 for dusting

FOR THE CUPCAKES

¾ cup (1½ sticks) unsalted butter,
 at room temperature

¾ cup plus 2 tablespoons superfine
 sugar

3 large eggs

1⅓ cups plus 1 tablespoon all-
 purpose flour, sifted

1¼ teaspoons baking powder

2 teaspoons vanilla extract

FOR THE TOPPING

1 teaspoon vanilla extract

2½ cups heavy cream, lightly
 whipped

¾ cup strawberries, sliced

sifted confectioners' sugar, for
 dusting

1. Preheat the oven to 350°F. Line a baking sheet with parchment paper. Line a 12-cup muffin pan with paper muffin liners.

2. For the shortbread, place the butter and sugar in a bowl and beat together until smooth. Stir in the flour to form a smooth dough. On a counter lightly dusted with flour, roll out the dough to a thickness of ½ inch. Using a 1½-inch flower cutter, stamp out 12 flowers. Place on the lined baking sheet.

3. Bake the shortbreads for 10–12 minutes until just starting to brown. Transfer to a wire rack to cool completely.

4. For the cakes, using a hand mixer, beat the butter and superfine sugar in a bowl, or beat with a wooden spoon, until pale and creamy. Gradually beat in the eggs until just combined.

5. Fold in the flour, baking powder, and vanilla extract and stir well to combine. Divide the batter evenly among the paper liners and bake for 15–20 minutes until risen and springy to the touch. Transfer to a wire rack to cool completely.

6. For the topping, stir the vanilla extract into the cream and transfer it to a pastry bag fitted with a plain large tip. Pipe a swirl of frosting on top of each cake and place a shortbread flower in the center of each cake. Arrange the sliced strawberries on the cream next to the shortbread. Dust with sifted confectioners' sugar.

Cherry Pie Cupcakes

Preparation Time 45 minutes • Cooking Time 25–30 minutes, plus cooling • Makes 12 •
Per Cupcake 432 calories, 31g fat (19g saturated), 37g carbohydrates, 400mg sodium • A Little Effort

FOR THE SHORTBREAD

¼ cup (½ stick) salted butter

2 tablespoons superfine sugar

½ cup all-purpose flour, plus extra
  for dusting

FOR THE CUPCAKES

¾ cup (1½ sticks) unsalted butter,
  at room temperature

¾ cup plus 2 tablespoons superfine
  sugar

3 large eggs

1⅓ cups plus 1 tablespoon all-
  purpose flour, sifted

1¼ teaspoons baking powder

2 teaspoons vanilla extract

FOR THE TOPPING

½ (14½-ounce) can pitted black
  cherries in syrup, drained,
  syrup reserved

1¼ cups heavy cream, lightly
  whipped

sifted confectioners' sugar, for
  dusting

1. Preheat the oven to 350°F. Line a baking sheet with parchment paper. Line a 12-cup muffin pan with paper muffin liners.

2. For the shortbread, place the butter and sugar in a bowl and beat together until smooth. Stir in the flour to form a smooth dough. On a counter lightly dusted with flour, roll out the dough to a thickness of ½ inch. Using a 1½-inch star cutter, stamp out 12 stars. Place on the lined baking sheet.

3. Bake the shortbreads for 10–12 minutes until just starting to brown. Transfer to a wire rack to cool completely.

4. For the cakes, using a hand mixer, beat the butter and superfine sugar in a bowl, or beat with a wooden spoon, until pale and creamy. Gradually beat in the eggs until just combined.

5. Fold in the flour, baking powder, and vanilla extract, and stir well to combine. Divide the batter evenly among the paper liners and bake for 15–20 minutes until risen and springy to the touch. Transfer to a wire rack to cool completely.

6. For the topping, set aside 12 of the cherries and finely chop the remainder. Stir the chopped cherries into the cream along with 2 tablespoons of the reserved syrup. Divide the cherry cream evenly among the cakes and top each with a shortbread star. Place one of the reserved cherries next to each star and dust with confectioners' sugar.

Rhubarb Custard Cupcakes

Preparation Time 35 minutes • Cooking Time 20–30 minutes, plus cooling • Makes 12 •
Per Cupcake 424 calories, 32g fat (18g saturated), 32g carbohydrates, 600mg sodium • A Little Effort

14 ounces rhubarb, chopped into ¾-inch pieces

4 tablespoons cold water

¾ cup plus 2 tablespoons superfine sugar, plus 2 tablespoons

¾ cup (1½ sticks) unsalted butter, at room temperature

3 large eggs

1⅓ cups plus 1 tablespoon all-purpose flour, sifted

1¼ teaspoons baking powder

2 teaspoons vanilla extract

FOR THE TOPPING

13 ounces ready-made fresh custard

2 cups mascarpone cheese

edible sugared rose petals, to decorate

1. Preheat the oven to 350°F. Line a 12-cup muffin pan with paper muffin liners.

2. Place the rhubarb in a small pan with the cold water and the 2 tablespoons sugar, and cook over medium heat for 5–10 minutes until the rhubarb is tender. Strain the rhubarb, reserving the syrup.

3. Using a hand mixer, beat the butter and superfine sugar in a bowl, or beat with a wooden spoon, until pale and creamy. Gradually beat in the eggs until just combined.

4. Fold in the flour, baking powder, vanilla, and 3 tablespoons of the reserved syrup and stir well to combine. Divide the batter evenly among the paper liners and bake for 15–20 minutes until risen and springy to the touch. Transfer to a wire rack to cool completely.

5. Using a cake plunger or a teaspoon, carefully remove a small piece of sponge from the center of each cake.

6. For the topping, combine the drained rhubarb with half the custard and stir well. Place the mascarpone cheese in a bowl and soften with a fork. Stir the remaining custard and 1 tablespoon of the reserved syrup into the mascarpone.

7. Just before serving, spoon a little of the rhubarb and custard mixture into the center of each cake. Transfer the mascarpone mixture to a pastry bag fitted with a large star tip and pipe around the edge of each cake. Decorate with the sugared rose petals.

Peaches and Cream Cupcakes

Preparation Time 30 minutes • Cooking Time 15–20 minutes, plus cooling • Makes 12 •
Per Cupcake 424 calories, 34g fat (18g saturated), 26g carbohydrates, 400mg sodium • Easy

¾ cup (1½ sticks) unsalted butter,
  at room temperature
¾ cup plus 2 tablespoons superfine
  sugar
3 large eggs
1 cup all-purpose flour, sifted
1 teaspoon baking powder
½ cup ground almonds

FOR THE TOPPING
1 cup mascarpone cheese
½ cup heavy cream, lightly
  whipped
2 ripe peaches, pitted and each
  sliced into 12
½ cup toasted slivered almonds

1. Preheat the oven to 350°F. Line a 12-cup muffin pan with paper muffin liners. Using a hand mixer, beat the butter and superfine sugar in a bowl, or beat with a wooden spoon, until pale and creamy. Gradually beat in the eggs until just combined.

2. Fold in the flour, baking powder, and almonds and stir well to combine. Divide the batter evenly among the paper liners and bake for 15–20 minutes until risen and springy to the touch. Transfer to a wire rack to cool completely.

3. For the topping, place the mascarpone in a bowl and soften with a fork. Stir in the heavy cream until smooth. Transfer the cream to a pastry bag fitted with a large tip and pipe the cream onto the cakes. Place 2 peach slices on each cake and sprinkle the almonds over.

Blood Orange Cupcakes

Preparation Time 35 minutes • Cooking Time 15–20 minutes, plus cooling • Makes 12 •
Per Cupcake 501 calories, 20g fat (12g saturated), 82g carbohydrates, 400mg sodium • Easy

¾ cup (1½ sticks) unsalted butter,
   at room temperature
¾ cup plus 2 tablespoons superfine
   sugar
3 large eggs
1⅓ cups plus 1 tablespoon all-
   purpose flour, sifted
1¼ teaspoons baking powder
2 blood oranges

FOR THE TOPPING
⅔ cup cream cheese
5¼ cups confectioners' sugar,
   sifted
finely grated zest and juice of
   1 unwaxed blood orange, plus
   orange zest to decorate (see
   Cook's Tip on page 162)

1. Preheat the oven to 350°F. Line a 12-cup muffin pan with paper muffin liners. Using a hand mixer, beat the butter and superfine sugar in a bowl, or beat with a wooden spoon, until pale and creamy. Gradually beat in the eggs until just combined.

2. Fold in the flour and baking powder, and grate the zest from the oranges in, stir well to combine. Divide the batter evenly among the paper liners and bake for 15–20 minutes until risen and springy to the touch. Transfer to a wire rack to cool completely.

3. For the topping, place the cream cheese in a medium bowl and stir with a fork to soften. Gradually add the sifted confectioners' sugar, stirring well until incorporated. Add the orange juice, enough to make a loose icing, plus the zest, and beat until well combined.

4. Spoon the icing onto each cake, spread to the edges with the back of a teaspoon, and top with some orange zest.

Pear and Toffee Cupcakes

Preparation Time 30 minutes • Cooking Time 15–20 minutes, plus cooling • Makes 12 •
Per Cupcake 495 calories, 36g fat (22g saturated), 42g carbohydrates, 600mg sodium • Easy

¾ cup (1½ sticks) unsalted butter,
  at room temperature
¾ cup plus 2 tablespoons packed
  light brown sugar
3 large eggs
1⅓ cups plus 1 tablespoon all-
  purpose flour, sifted
1¼ teaspoons baking powder
1½ teaspoons ground nutmeg
2 pears, peeled, cored, and very
  finely chopped
4 tablespoons toffee sauce

FOR THE TOPPING
1 cup mascarpone cheese
1 cup heavy cream
4 tablespoons toffee sauce
1½ ounces toffee, finely chopped

1. Preheat the oven to 350°F. Line a 12-cup muffin pan with paper muffin liners. Using a hand mixer, beat the butter and light brown sugar in a bowl, or beat with a wooden spoon, until pale and creamy. Gradually beat in the eggs until just combined.

2. Fold in the flour, baking powder, nutmeg, chopped pears, and toffee sauce, and stir well to combine. Divide the batter evenly among the paper liners and bake for 15–20 minutes until risen and springy to the touch. Transfer to a wire rack to cool completely.

3. For the topping, place the mascarpone cheese and cream in a bowl and beat together until well combined. Stir in the toffee sauce. Transfer the frosting to a pastry bag fitted with a large star tip and pipe swirls of frosting on top of each cake. Sprinkle the chopped toffee over.

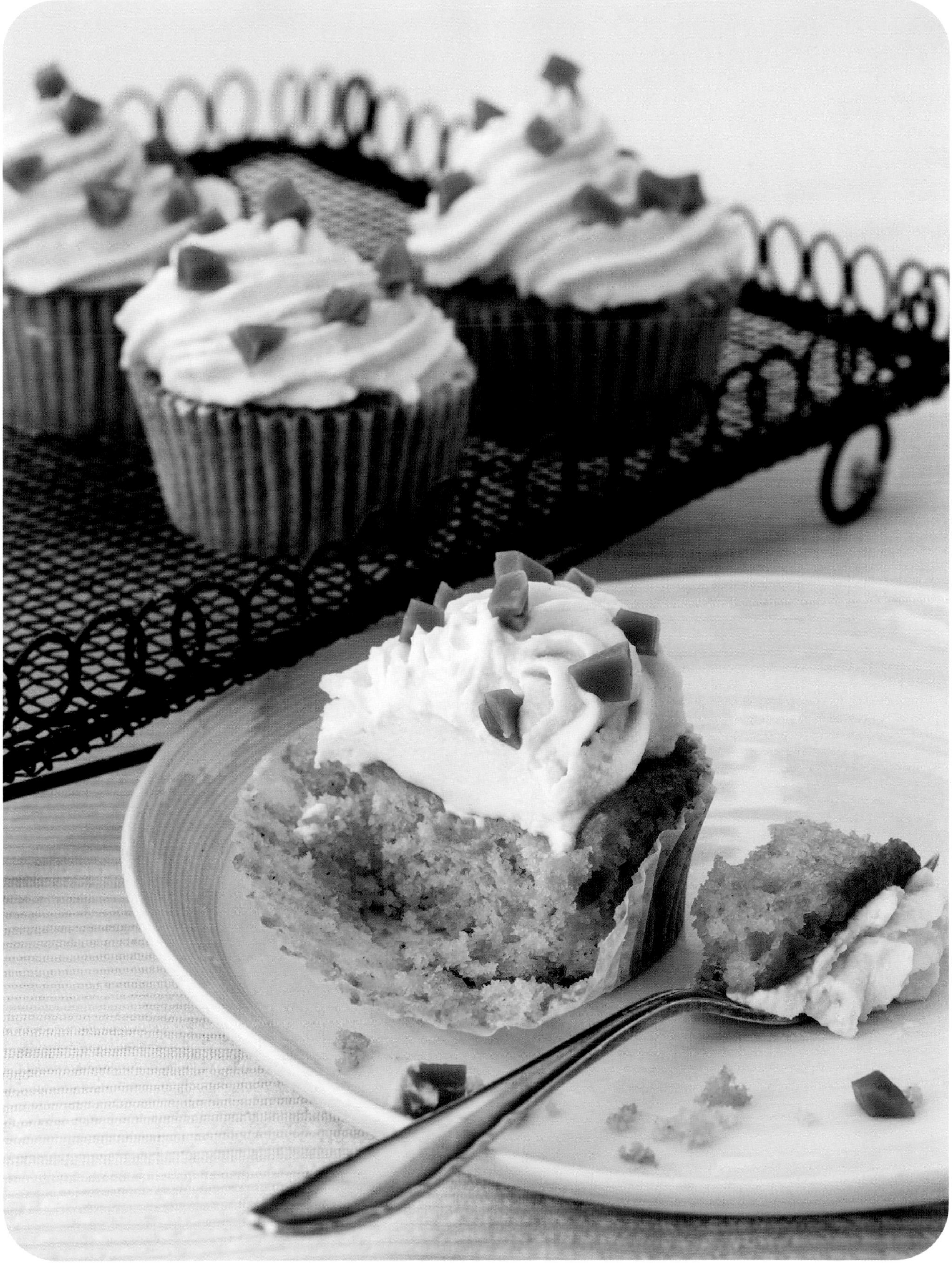

Mango and Passion Fruit Cupcakes

Preparation Time 30 minutes • Cooking Time 25 minutes, plus cooling • Makes 12 • Per Cupcake 374 calories, 18g fat (11g saturated), 52g carbohydrates, 400mg sodium • Easy

4 ripe passion fruit
⅓ cup orange juice
10 tablespoons unsalted butter, softened
2 cups all-purpose flour, sifted
¾ cup plus 2 tablespoons superfine sugar
3 large eggs
1 tablespoon baking powder
3 ounces ready-to-eat dried mango, finely chopped

FOR THE TOPPING
½ cup cream cheese
2 tablespoons unsalted butter, softened
1¾ cups confectioners' sugar, sifted
1 large, ripe passion fruit
white sugar sprinkles

1. Preheat the oven to 350°F. Line a 12-cup muffin pan with paper muffin liners.

2. Cut the passion fruit in half and pass the seeds and juice through a strainer into a bowl. Discard the seeds. Add enough orange juice to make ½ cup liquid.

3. Put the butter, flour, superfine sugar, eggs, baking powder, passion fruit, and orange juice into a large bowl. Using a hand mixer or wooden spoon, beat together until pale and creamy. Add the chopped mango and fold through until combined. Divide the batter equally between the paper liners.

4. Bake for 25 minutes or until golden and risen. Leave to cool in the pan for 5 minutes, and then transfer to a wire rack to cool completely.

5. For the topping, beat together the cream cheese and butter until fluffy. Gradually add the confectioners' sugar until combined. Cut the passion fruit in half and pass the seeds and juice through a strainer into the frosting. Discard the seeds. Stir to combine, and then, using a small spatula, spread a little over the top of each cake. Scatter on the sugar sprinkles.

TO STORE
Store in an airtight container in the fridge. They will keep for 2–3 days.

FREEZING TIP
To freeze Complete the recipe to the end of step 4. Open-freeze, and then wrap and freeze.
To use Thaw for about 1 hour, and then complete the recipe.

Sour Cherry Cupcakes

Preparation Time 30 minutes • Cooking Time 15–20 minutes, plus cooling and setting • Makes 12 •
Per Cupcake 323 calories, 14g fat (8g saturated), 50g carbohydrates, 400mg sodium • Easy

¾ cup (1½ sticks) unsalted butter, softened

¾ cup plus 2 tablespoons superfine sugar

3 large eggs

1⅓ cups plus 1 tablespoon all-purpose flour, sifted

1¼ teaspoons baking powder

3 ounces dried cherries

2 tablespoons milk

FOR THE TOPPING

2 cups confectioners' sugar, sifted

3 tablespoons lemon juice, strained

1. Preheat the oven to 375°F. Line a 12-cup muffin pan with paper muffin liners.

2. Put the butter and superfine sugar into a bowl and cream together until pale, light, and fluffy. Beat in the eggs, one at a time, folding in 1 tablespoon flour if the mixture looks like it is starting to curdle.

3. Put 12 dried cherries to one side. Fold the remaining flour, the cherries, and milk into the creamed batter until evenly combined. Spoon the batter into the paper liners and bake for 15–20 minutes until pale golden and risen. Transfer to a wire rack to cool completely.

4. For the topping, put the confectioners' sugar into a bowl and mix with the lemon juice to make a smooth dropping consistency. Spoon a little icing onto each cake and decorate each with a cherry. Then stand the cakes upright on a wire rack and leave for about 1 hour to set.

TO STORE
Store in an airtight container. They will keep for 3–5 days.

FREEZING TIP
To freeze *Complete the recipe to the end of step 3. Open-freeze, and then wrap and freeze.*
To use *Thaw for about 1 hour, and then complete the recipe.*

MUFFIN
MEDLEY

Lemon Poppy Seed Muffins

Preparation Time 30 minutes • Cooking Time 15–20 minutes, plus cooling • Makes 12 •
Per Muffin 149 calories, 7g fat (1g saturated), 27g carbohydrates, 300mg sodium • A Little Effort

1½ cups plus 2 tablespoons all-
   purpose flour
1½ teaspoons baking powder
½ cup superfine sugar
zest of 2 unwaxed lemons (see
   Cook's Tip on page 162)
5 tablespoons poppy seeds
¼ cup sunflower oil
⅓ cup plus 1 tablespoon milk
1 large egg
juice of 1 lemon
sifted confectioners' sugar, for
   dusting
12 teaspoons lemon curd
edible violas, to decorate (optional)

1. Preheat the oven to 350°F. Line a 12-cup muffin pan with paper muffin liners.

2. Place the flour, baking powder, sugar, lemon zest and 3 tablespoons of the poppy seeds in a large bowl. In another bowl, place the oil, milk, egg, and lemon juice. Stir together with a fork until well combined. Pour the egg mixture into the dry ingredients and mix well.

3. Divide the batter evenly among the paper liners. Bake for 20–25 minutes until golden and springy to the touch. Transfer to a wire rack to cool.

4. Dust each muffin with confectioners' sugar and spoon 1 teaspoon of lemon curd over the top of each. Sprinkle the remaining poppy seeds over each muffin and decorate with an edible viola, if desired.

Banana and Pecan Muffins

Preparation Time 10 minutes • Cooking Time 20 minutes • Makes 12 • Per Muffin 236 calories,
9g fat (4g saturated), 37g carbohydrates, 800mg sodium • Easy

2¾ cups plus 1 tablespoon all-
   purpose flour
2½ teaspoons baking powder
1 tablespoon baking soda
1 teaspoon salt
3 very ripe large bananas, peeled
   and mashed
⅔ cup superfine sugar
1 extra-large egg
2 tablespoons milk
⅓ cup butter, melted
½ cup chopped roasted pecan nuts

1. Preheat the oven to 350°F. Line a 12-cup muffin pan with 12 paper muffin liners. Sift together the flour, baking powder, baking soda, and salt, and put to one side.

2. Combine the bananas, sugar, egg, and milk, and then pour in the melted butter and mix well. Add to the flour mixture with the nuts, stirring quickly and gently with just a few strokes. Fill the muffin liners halfway.

3. Bake for 20 minutes or until golden and risen. Transfer to a wire rack and leave to cool.

COOK'S TIP
The secret to really light, fluffy muffins is a light hand, so be sure to sift the flour. Stir the mixture as little as possible; it's okay if it looks a little lumpy. Overmixing will give tough, chewy results.

Whole-Wheat Banana Muffins

Preparation Time 15 minutes, plus soaking • Cooking Time 20–25 minutes • Makes 6 • Per Muffin 341 calories, 13g fat (2g saturated), 51g carbohydrates, 600mg sodium • Easy

¼ cup plus 2 teaspoons raisins
**finely grated zest and juice of
1 unwaxed orange (see Cook's
Tip on page 162)**
**¾ cup plus 1 tablespoon whole-
wheat flour**
¼ cup wheat germ
3 tablespoons superfine sugar
2 teaspoons baking powder
a pinch of salt
1 extra-large egg, beaten
⅛ cup plus 1 tablespoon milk
**⅛ cup plus 1 tablespoon sunflower
oil**
**2 medium ripe bananas, roughly
mashed**

FOR THE TOPPING
5 tablespoons orange marmalade
**2 ounces banana chips, roughly
chopped**
½ cup walnuts, roughly chopped

1. Preheat the oven to 400°F. Line a 6-cup muffin pan with paper muffin liners. Put the raisins into a bowl, pour the orange juice over them, and leave to soak for 1 hour.

2. Put the orange zest into a bowl with the flour, wheat germ, sugar, baking powder, and salt, and mix together. Make a well in the center.

3. In a separate bowl, mix the egg, milk, and oil. Pour into the flour mixture and stir until just blended. Drain the raisins, reserving 1 tablespoon of the juice, and stir into the mixture with the bananas. Don't overmix. Fill each muffin liner two-thirds full.

4. Bake for 20–25 minutes until a toothpick inserted into the center comes out clean. Transfer to a wire rack to cool slightly.

5. For the topping, gently heat the marmalade with the reserved orange juice until melted. Simmer for 1 minute, and then add the banana chips and walnuts. Spoon on top of the muffins. Serve while still warm.

FREEZING TIP
To freeze *Complete the recipe to the end of step 4. Once the muffins are cool, you can pack, seal, and freeze them.*
To use *Thaw at room temperature. Complete the recipe.*

Blueberry Muffins

Preparation Time 10 minutes • Cooking Time 20–25 minutes, plus cooling • Makes 12 • Per Muffin 218 calories, 2g fat (trace saturated), 49g carbohydrates, 500mg sodium • Easy

2 large eggs

1 cup plus 2 tablespoons low-fat milk

1¼ cups granulated sugar

2 teaspoons vanilla extract

2¾ cups plus 1 tablespoon all-purpose flour

4 teaspoons baking powder

1¾ cups frozen blueberries

finely grated zest of 2 unwaxed lemons (see Cook's Tip on page 162)

1. Preheat the oven to 400°F. Line a 12-cup muffin pan with paper muffin liners.

2. Put the eggs, milk, sugar, and vanilla extract into a bowl and mix well.

3. In another bowl, sift the flour and baking powder together, and then add the blueberries and lemon zest. Toss together and make a well in the center.

4. Pour the egg mixture into the flour and blueberries, and mix in gently—overmixing will make the muffins tough. Divide the batter equally between the paper liners.

5. Bake for 20–25 minutes until risen and just firm. Transfer to a wire rack to cool completely. These are best eaten on the day they are made.

FREEZING TIP

To freeze Complete the recipe. Once the muffins are cool, you can pack, seal, and freeze them.
To use Thaw at room temperature.

Wheat-free Blueberry Muffins

Preparation Time 15 minutes • Cooking Time 15 minutes • Makes 12 • Per Muffin 228 calories, 8g fat (3g saturated), 36g carbohydrates, 100mg sodium

2¼ cups rice flour

2 teaspoons wheat-free baking powder

1 teaspoon baking soda

½ cup plus 2 tablespoons superfine sugar

¾ cup ground almonds (almond meal)

finely grated zest of 1 unwaxed lemon (see Cook's Tip on page 162)

¾ cup dried blueberries

1 large egg

1 teaspoon vanilla extract

1 cup skim milk

½ stick (¼ cup) unsalted butter, melted

1. Preheat the oven to 400°F. Line a 12-cup muffin pan with 12 paper muffin liners.

2. Put the flour, baking powder, and baking soda into a bowl. Then stir in the superfine sugar, ground almonds, lemon zest, and dried blueberries.

3. Put the egg, vanilla extract, milk, and butter into a bowl and mix together with a fork. Pour this liquid into the dry ingredients and lightly fold together.

4. Divide the batter equally between the paper liners. Bake in the oven for 15 minutes or until the muffins are risen, pale golden, and just firm.

5. Transfer the muffins to a wire rack to cool slightly before serving.

Bran and Apple Muffins

Preparation Time 20 minutes • Cooking Time 30 minutes • Makes 10 • Per Muffin 137 calories,
1g fat (trace saturated), 31g carbohydrates, 300mg sodium • Easy

1 cup plus 2 tablespoons low-fat milk

2 tablespoons orange juice

1 cup bran flakes cereal

9 dried prunes

½ cup water

½ cup packed light brown sugar

2 large egg whites

1 tablespoon light corn syrup

1⅛ cups plus 4 teaspoons all-purpose flour, sifted

1 teaspoon baking powder

1 teaspoon ground cinnamon

1 Pippin apple, peeled and grated

raw sugar to sprinkle

1. Preheat the oven to 375°F. Line a muffin pan with 10 paper muffin liners.

2. In a bowl, mix the milk and orange juice with the cereal. Put to one side for 10 minutes.

3. Put the prunes into a food processor or blender with the water and process for 2–3 minutes to make a puree. Add the brown sugar and process briefly to mix.

4. Put the egg whites into a clean, grease-free bowl and whisk until soft peaks form. Add the whites to the milk mixture with the syrup, flour, baking powder, cinnamon, grated apple, and prune mixture. Fold all the ingredients together gently—don't overmix.

5. Divide the batter equally between the paper liners. Bake for 30 minutes or until well risen and golden brown. Transfer to a wire rack to cool. Sprinkle with raw sugar just before serving. These are best eaten on the day they are made.

FREEZING TIP

To freeze *Complete the recipe, but don't sprinkle with the sugar topping. Once the muffins are cool, you can pack, seal, and freeze.*
To use *Thaw at room temperature. Sprinkle with the sugar to serve.*

Brown Sugar Muffins

Preparation Time 10 minutes • Cooking Time 30–35 minutes, plus cooling • Makes 6 • Per Muffin 233 calories, 8g fat (5g saturated), 38g carbohydrates, 400mg sodium • Easy

1⅛ cups plus 4 teaspoons all-purpose flour

1½ teaspoons baking powder

¼ teaspoon salt

1 large egg, beaten

⅛ cup plus 4 teaspoons superfine sugar

4 tablespoons unsalted butter, melted

½ teaspoon vanilla extract

⅓ cup plus 1 tablespoon milk

2 tablespoons brown sugar

1. Preheat the oven to 400°F. Line a 6-cup muffin pan with paper muffin liners.

2. Sift the flour, baking powder, and salt together.

3. Put the beaten egg, superfine sugar, melted butter, vanilla extract, and milk into a large bowl and stir to combine. Gently fold in the sifted flour. Spoon the batter equally into the paper liners and sprinkle with the brown sugar.

4. Bake for 30–35 minutes until golden. Transfer to a wire rack to cool completely. These are best eaten on the day they are made.

FREEZING TIP

To freeze Complete the recipe. Once the muffins are cool, you can pack, seal, and freeze.
To use Thaw at room temperature.

Double Chocolate Muffins

Preparation Time 20 minutes • Cooking Time 30 minutes • Makes 12 • Per Muffin 370 calories, 19g fat (11g saturated), 47g carbohydrates, 0mg sodium • Easy

½ cup (1 stick) unsalted butter, cut into cubes

3½ ounces semisweet chocolate, chopped

2⅛ cups plus 4 teaspoons all-purpose flour

1 teaspoon baking soda

⅓ cup unsweetened cocoa powder

¾ cup plus 2 tablespoons superfine sugar

7 ounces white chocolate, chopped

a pinch of salt

1 large egg

¾ cup plus 1 tablespoon milk

½ cup plain yogurt

1 teaspoon vanilla extract

1. Preheat the oven to 375°F. Line a 12-cup muffin pan with paper muffin liners.

2. Melt the butter and chocolate in a heatproof bowl over a pot of barely simmering water, making sure the bottom of the bowl doesn't touch the water. Mix together very gently, and then leave to cool a little.

3. Put the flour into a large bowl. Add the baking soda, cocoa powder, sugar, white chocolate, and a pinch of salt. Stir everything together. Beat together the egg, milk, yogurt, and vanilla in a bowl.

4. Pour both the egg mix and the chocolate mix onto the dry ingredients, and then roughly fold together. Be careful not to overmix the ingredients or the muffins will be tough and won't rise properly.

5. Divide the mixture among the prepared muffin liners. Bake for 20–25 minutes until well risen and springy. Remove from the pan, still in their liners, and cool on a wire rack.

Strawberry and Chocolate Muffins

Preparation Time 25 minutes • Cooking Time 30 minutes • Makes 4 • Per Muffin 420 calories, 20g fat (12g saturated), 55g carbohydrates, 600mg sodium • Easy

2 Double Chocolate Muffins (see page 216), halved

4 tablespoons mascarpone cheese, softened

5 cups strawberries, hulled and roughly chopped

semisweet chocolate (at least 70% cocoa solids), grated, to decorate

1. Divide the muffin halves among four plates. Top each half with a tablespoon of the mascarpone and a good spoonful of strawberries.

2. Sprinkle with the grated chocolate, and serve immediately.

Chocolate Banana Muffins

Preparation Time 15 minutes • Cooking Time 20 minutes, plus cooling • Makes 12 • Per Muffin 228 calories
7g fat (4g saturated), 40g carbohydrates, 500mg sodium • Easy

2⅛ cups plus 4 teaspoons all-purpose flour

2½ teaspoons baking soda

½ teaspoon salt

3 large ripe bananas

½ cup plus 2 tablespoons superfine sugar

1 extra-large egg, beaten

⅛ cup plus 1 tablespoon low-fat milk

6 tablespoons unsalted butter, melted and cooled

2 ounces semisweet chocolate, chopped

1. Preheat the oven to 350°F. Line a 12-cup muffin pan with paper muffin liners.

2. Sift the flour, baking soda, and salt together into a large mixing bowl and put to one side.

3. Peel the bananas and mash with a fork in a bowl. Add the superfine sugar, egg, milk, and melted butter, and mix until well combined. Add this to the flour mixture, with the chopped chocolate. Stir gently, using only a few strokes, until the flour is only just incorporated—do not overmix. The batter should be lumpy. Spoon the batter into the liners.

4. Bake for 20 minutes or until the muffins are well risen and golden. Transfer to a wire rack to cool completely. These are best eaten on the day they are made.

FREEZING TIP

To freeze Complete the recipe. Once the muffins are cool, you can pack, seal, and freeze.
To use Thaw at cool room temperature.

Spiced Carrot Muffins

Preparation Time 30 minutes • Cooking Time 20–25 minutes, plus cooling • Makes 12 • Per Muffin 333 calories, 22g fat (11g saturated), 31g carbohydrates, 500mg sodium • Easy

1 stick (½ cup) unsalted butter, softened

½ cup plus 2 tablespoons packed light brown sugar

3 pieces of preserved ginger, drained and chopped

1⅛ cups plus 4 teaspoons all-purpose flour, sifted

2½ teaspoons baking powder

1 tablespoon apple pie spice

¼ cup plus 2 tablespoons ground almonds (almond meal)

3 large eggs

finely grated zest of ½ unwaxed orange (see Cook's Tip on page 162)

2–3 small carrots (about 5 ounces), grated

⅓ cup pecan nuts, chopped

¼ cup plus 2 tablespoons golden raisins

3 tablespoons white rum or orange liqueur* (optional)

FOR THE TOPPING

1 cup cream cheese

⅔ cup confectioners' sugar

1 teaspoon lemon juice

12 unsprayed rose petals (optional)

1. Preheat the oven to 350°F. Line a 12-cup muffin pan with paper muffin liners.

2. Beat the butter, brown sugar, and preserved ginger together until pale and creamy. Add the flour, baking powder, spice, ground almonds, eggs, and orange zest, and beat well until combined. Stir in the carrots, pecan nuts, and golden raisins. Divide the batter equally among the paper liners.

3. Bake for 20–25 minutes until risen and just firm. A toothpick inserted into the center should come out clean. Transfer to a wire rack and cool completely.

4. For the topping, beat the cream cheese in a bowl until softened. Beat in the confectioners' sugar and lemon juice to give a smooth icing that just holds its shape.

5. Drizzle each cake with a little liqueur, if using. Using a small spatula, spread a little icing over each cake. Decorate with a rose petal, if you like.

* This recipe is not suitable for children if it contains alcohol.

TO STORE

Store in an airtight container. They will keep for up to one week.

FREEZING TIP

To freeze Complete the recipe to the end of step 3. Once the muffins are cool, you can pack, seal, and freeze them.

To use Thaw at room temperature and complete the recipe.

Honey and Yogurt Muffins

Preparation Time 15 minutes • Cooking Time 17–20 minutes • Makes 12 • Per Muffin 180 calories, 6g fat (4g saturated), 27g carbohydrates, 100mg sodium • Easy

1¾ cups plus 1 tablespoon all-purpose flour

1½ teaspoons baking powder

1 teaspoon baking soda

½ teaspoon apple pie spice

½ teaspoon ground nutmeg

a pinch of salt

½ cup ground oatmeal

¼ cup packed light brown sugar

1 cup plain Greek yogurt

½ cup milk

1 egg

4 tablespoons butter, melted and cooled

4 tablespoons honey

1. Preheat the oven to 400°F. Line a 12-cup muffin pan with paper muffin liners.

2. Sift the flour, baking powder, baking soda, apple pie spice, nutmeg, and salt into a bowl. Stir in the oatmeal and brown sugar.

3. Mix the yogurt with the milk in a bowl. Then beat in the egg, butter, and honey. Pour onto the dry ingredients and stir in quickly until just blended—don't overmix. Divide the batter equally between the paper liners.

4. Bake for 17–20 minutes until the muffins are well risen and just firm. Leave to cool in the pan for 5 minutes, and then transfer to a wire rack. These are best eaten on the day they are made.

FREEZING TIP

To freeze Complete the recipe. Once the muffins are cool, you can pack, seal, and freeze them.
To use Thaw at room temperature.

Candied Cherry and Almond Muffins

Preparation Time 10 minutes • Cooking Time 25 minutes plus cooling • Makes 12 • Per Muffin 230 calories, 6g fat (1g saturated), 42g carbohydrates, 100mg sodium • Easy

1¾ cups plus 1 tablespoon all-purpose flour

1 teaspoon baking powder

a pinch of salt

⅓ cup superfine sugar

½ cup ground almonds (almond meal)

1½ cups candied cherries, roughly chopped

1¼ cups milk

3 tablespoons lemon juice

3 tablespoons sunflower oil or melted butter

1 large egg

1 teaspoon almond extract

roughly crushed sugar cubes to decorate

1. Preheat the oven to 375°F. Line a 12-cup muffin pan with paper muffin liners.

2. Sift the flour, baking powder, and salt together. Add the superfine sugar and ground almonds, and then stir in the chopped cherries.

3. Whisk the milk, lemon juice, oil or butter, the egg, and almond extract together. Pour into the dry ingredients and stir until all the ingredients are just combined—the mixture should be lumpy. Do not over-mix or the muffins will be tough. Spoon the mixture equally into the paper liners and sprinkle with the crushed sugar cubes.

4. Bake for about 25 minutes or until golden and well risen.

5. Leave to cool in the pan for 5 minutes, and then transfer to a wire rack to cool completely. These are best eaten on the day they are made.

FREEZING TIP

To freeze Complete the recipe. Once the muffins are cool, you can pack, seal, and freeze them.
To use Thaw at room temperature.

New Potato, Pea, and Mint Frittata Muffins

Preparation Time 15 minutes • Cooking Time 40 minutes • Makes 12 (serves 6) • Per Muffin 160 calories, 12g fat (4g saturated), 6g carbohydrates, 90mg sodium • Easy

3 tablespoons olive oil, plus extra to grease
⅔ cup freshly grated Parmesan cheese
5 ounces baby new potatoes, roughly chopped
1 cup fresh peas, shelled
2 red onions, cut into thin wedges
1 tablespoon chopped fresh mint
8 large eggs
⅔ cup light cream
salt and black pepper

1. Preheat the oven to 350°F. Lightly oil a deep 12-cup nonstick muffin pan. Sprinkle a pinch of grated Parmesan into each cup.

2. Put the potatoes in a pan of cold, salted water. Bring to a boil and cook for about 5 minutes or until just tender. Add the peas to the potatoes for the last 3 minutes of cooking time. Drain well.

3. Heat the olive oil in a large nonstick frying pan and fry the onions for 7–10 minutes until soft and golden. Add the drained vegetables and the chopped mint. Cook, stirring, for 1 minute. Set aside to cool.

4. Beat the eggs in a large bowl with the cream and half the remaining Parmesan. Season well with salt and black pepper.

5. Divide the vegetables equally among the muffin cups, and then pour in the egg mix until nearly full. Sprinkle with remaining cheese. Cook for 20–25 minutes or until just set and golden. Cool in the pan for 20 minutes. Then run a knife around the edge of each frittata and turn out onto a board. Serve when cooled to room temperature.

FREEZING TIP

To freeze Complete the recipe. Once the frittatas are cool, put them in an airtight container and freeze for up to one month.
To use Thaw overnight in the fridge, taking them out about one hour before you're ready to serve.

Mini Bacon and Cheese Muffins

Preparation Time 15 minutes • Cooking Time 18 minutes • Makes 24 minis •
Per Muffin 43 calories, 2g fat (1g saturated), 5g carbohydrates, 78mg sodium • Easy

3 slices bacon, finely chopped

1⅓ cups plus 1 tablespoon all-purpose flour

1¼ teaspoons baking powder

½ cup finely grated mature cheddar cheese

1 teaspoon mustard powder

salt and black pepper, to taste

1 extra-large egg

½ cup milk

1. Preheat oven to 375°F and line a 24-cup mini muffin pan with paper muffin liners. Heat a frying pan over medium heat and fry the bacon until crisp and golden. Drain on paper towels.

2. In a medium bowl, mix together the flour, baking powder, most of the cheese, the mustard powder, and the salt and pepper. In a separate bowl, mix together the egg, milk, and cooked bacon. Add the wet ingredients to the dry bowl and mix until just combined (do not overmix or the muffins will be tough).

3. Divide the mixture among the liners and sprinkle with the remaining cheese. Bake for 12 minutes or until golden and springy to the touch. Serve warm or at room temperature.

GET AHEAD
Make the recipe up to 3 hours ahead. Leave at room temperature until ready to serve.

Cheesy Spinach Muffins

Preparation Time 15 minutes • Cooking Time 12–15 minutes • Makes 6 • Per Muffin 204 calories,
10g fat (6g saturated), 20g carbohydrates, 800mg sodium • Easy

3½ ounces baby spinach

1⅓ cups plus 1 tablespoon all-
purpose flour

2¼ teaspoons baking powder

⅓ cup grated Parmesan cheese

½ cup finely cubed cheddar
cheese

salt and ground black pepper

2 tablespoons butter, melted

⅓ cup plus 1 tablespoon milk

2 large eggs

a small handful of fresh parsley,
finely chopped

1. Preheat the oven to 400°F. Line six cups in a 12-cup muffin pan with paper muffin liners. Put the spinach into a strainer and pour boiling water over the spinach until it wilts. Leave the spinach to cool, and then squeeze out as much water as you can before finely chopping it. Put to one side.

2. In a large bowl, mix together the flour, baking powder, most of the Parmesan and cheddar cheeses, and some salt and pepper.

3. In a separate bowl, whisk together the butter, milk, eggs, parsley, and chopped spinach. Quickly mix the wet ingredients into the dry. Don't worry if there are floury lumps, as these will cook out.

4. Divide the mixture evenly among the paper liners, and then sprinkle with the remaining cheeses. Cook for 12–15 minutes until the muffins are risen, golden, and cooked through. Serve warm.

GET AHEAD

Prepare the muffins to the end of step 2 up to one day in advance. Put the chopped spinach into a bowl, cover, and chill. Cover the flour and cheese mixture and chill, and then complete the recipe to serve.

Smoked Salmon and Cream Cheese Muffins

Preparation Time 15 minutes • Cooking Time 20–25 minutes, plus cooling • Makes 12 •
Per Muffin 250 calories, 17g fat (8g saturated), 17g carbohydrates, 1,200mg sodium • Easy

1¾ cups plus 1 tablespoon all-
purpose flour

½ cup oats

2 teaspoons baking powder

salt and freshly ground black
pepper

½ teaspoon baking soda

½ ounce snipped chives plus extra
to garnish

½ cup plus 2 tablespoons grated
Parmesan cheese

zest of 1 unwaxed lemon (see
Cook's Tip on page 162)

2 eggs

1 cup plus 2 tablespoons plain
Greek yogurt

4 tablespoons olive oil

2 tablespoons milk

¾ cup plus 1 tablespoon cream
cheese

3½ ounces smoked salmon, cut
into bite-size pieces

1. Preheat the oven to 350°F. Line a 12-cup muffin pan with paper muffin liners. Place the flour, oats, baking powder, baking soda, chives, ½ cup of the Parmesan, lemon zest, and seasoning in a large bowl. Stir well to combine.

2. Place the eggs, yogurt, olive oil, and milk in a bowl and stir well with a fork until combined. Pour the egg mixture into the dry ingredients and stir until well mixed. Divide the batter evenly among the paper liners, sprinkle with the 2 tablespoons Parmesan, and bake for 20–25 minutes until risen and springy to the touch. Transfer to a wire rack to cool for 10 minutes.

3. Cut a cross in the top of each warm muffin and spoon in some of the cream cheese. Top with some salmon, snipped chives, and freshly ground black pepper. Serve at room temperature.

Tomato, Olive, and Basil Muffins

Preparation Time 10 minutes • Cooking Time 15–20 minutes, plus cooling • Makes 12 •
Per Muffin 128 calories, 4g fat (2g saturated), 19g carbohydrates, 1,000mg sodium • Easy

2⅛ cups plus 4 teaspoons all-
    purpose flour
2 teaspoons baking powder
salt and freshly ground black
    pepper
¾ cup milk
2 large eggs
6 tablespoons butter, melted
2 tablespoons plain yogurt
14 cherry tomatoes, halved
⅓ cup plus 1 tablespoon pitted
    black olives, halved
3½ ounces feta cheese, cubed
2 teaspoons dried basil
handful of fresh basil leaves,
    chopped, plus extra to garnish
    (optional)

1. Preheat the oven to 350°F. Line a 12-cup muffin pan with paper muffin liners. Sift the flour and baking powder into a large bowl and season well with salt and pepper.

2. In a large bowl, place the milk, eggs, melted butter, and yogurt. Stir with a fork until well combined. Pour into the flour and mix together.

3. Fold in the tomatoes, olives, feta, and dried and fresh basil. Divide the batter evenly among the paper liners. Bake for 15–20 minutes until golden and springy to the touch. Transfer to a wire rack to cool completely. Garnish with fresh basil leaves to serve, if liked.

Parmesan and Sun-Dried Tomatoes Muffins

Preparation Time 15 minutes • Cooking Time 20–25 minutes, plus cooling • Makes 12 •
Per Muffin 215 calories, 13g fat (3g saturated), 19g carbohydrates, 1,100mg sodium • Easy

1 (10-ounce) jar sun-dried tomatoes
   in oil
2⅛ cups plus 4 teaspoons all-
   purpose flour
1 tablespoon baking powder
1¼ cups grated Parmesan cheese
1 teaspoon fresh rosemary
½ teaspoon dried chili flakes
   (optional)
salt and freshly ground black
   pepper
⅓ cup plus 1 tablespoon milk
⅓ cup plus 1 tablespoon
   buttermilk
2 large eggs

1. Preheat the oven to 350°F. Line a 12-cup muffin pan with paper muffin liners. Drain the tomatoes, reserving the oil. Finely chop the tomatoes.

2. Sift the flour and baking powder into a large bowl. Stir in 1 cup of the Parmesan, the rosemary, chili, and chopped tomatoes. Season well with salt and pepper.

3. In a large bowl, place the milk, buttermilk, eggs, and ½ cup of the reserved oil. Stir with a fork until well combined. Pour into the dry ingredients and mix together. Divide the batter evenly among the paper liners and sprinkle the remaining cheese over. Bake for 20–25 minutes until golden and springy to the touch. Transfer to a wire rack to cool completely. Serve at room temperature.

Ham and Cheese Muffins

Preparation Time 15 minutes • Cooking Time 15–20 minutes, plus cooling • Makes 12 •
Per Muffin 216 calories, 12g fat (4g saturated), 19g carbohydrates, 1,000mg sodium • Easy

3½ ounces prosciutto

2⅛ cups plus 4 teaspoons all-
purpose flour

1 tablespoon baking powder

1¼ cups mature cheddar cheese,
grated

3 tablespoons snipped chives plus
extra to garnish

salt and freshly ground black
pepper

¾ cup plus 1 tablespoon milk

2 large eggs

⅓ cup plus 1 tablespoon sunflower
oil

1. Preheat the oven to 350°F. Line a 12-cup muffin pan with paper muffin liners. Place the prosciutto in a large nonstick skillet, in a single layer, over high heat and cook until crispy, turning once. Remove and let cool and drain on paper towels.

2. Sift the flour and baking powder into a large bowl. Stir in 1 cup of the cheese and the chives. Season well. Snip the crispy ham into small pieces using kitchen scissors, and add to the mixture.

3. In a large bowl, place the milk, eggs, and oil. Stir with a fork until well combined. Pour into the dry ingredients and mix together.

4. Divide the batter evenly among the paper liners and sprinkle the remaining cheese over. Bake for 15–20 minutes until golden and springy to the touch. Transfer to a wire rack to cool completely. Garnish with snipped chives and serve at room temperature.

Spinach and Ricotta Muffins

Preparation Time 15 minutes • Cooking Time 25–30 minutes, plus cooling • Makes 12 •
Per Muffin 208 calories, 14g fat (4g saturated), 14g carbohydrates, 600mg sodium • Easy

3½ ounces baby spinach

1½ cups plus 2 tablespoons all-
  purpose flour

1½ teaspoons baking powder

1¼ cups grated Parmesan cheese

½ teaspoon grated nutmeg

salt and freshly ground black
  pepper

⅓ cup plus 1 tablespoon
  buttermilk

⅓ cup plus 1 tablespoon vegetable
  oil

¾ cup ricotta cheese

2 eggs

¼ cup toasted pine nuts

1. Preheat the oven to 350°F. Line a 12-cup muffin pan with paper muffin liners.

2. Place the spinach in a large bowl and pour over enough water from a just boiled kettle to cover. Let wilt for 1 minute. Transfer to a colander, drain, and press out any excess water. Chop the spinach.

3. Sift the flour and baking powder into a large bowl. Stir in 1 cup of the cheese and the nutmeg and season well with salt and pepper.

4. In a large bowl, place the buttermilk, vegetable oil, ricotta, and eggs. Stir well with a fork until well combined. Pour into the dry ingredients, along with the chopped spinach and pine nuts, and mix together.

5. Divide the batter evenly among the paper liners and sprinkle the remaining cheese over. Bake for 25–30 minutes until golden and springy to the touch. Transfer to a wire rack to cool completely.

Index